JUICE

JUICE

over **100** **nutritious** juices
& smoothies to **rehydrate,**
soothe & energize

This edition published by Parragon Books Ltd in 2016
and distributed by

Parragon Inc.
440 Park Avenue South, 13th Floor
New York, NY 10016
www.parragon.com/lovefood

LOVE FOOD is an imprint of Parragon Books Ltd

ISBN 978-1-4748-1753-0

Printed in China

Introduction by Fiona Hunter
New recipes by Jane Hughes
New photography by Tony Briscoe and Al Richardson
Production by Fiona Rhys-Griffith
Designed by Beth Kalynka

Notes for the Reader
This book uses standard kitchen measuring spoons and cups. All spoon and cup measurements are level unless otherwise indicated. Unless otherwise stated, milk is assumed to be whole, eggs are large, individual vegetables are medium, and pepper is freshly ground black pepper. Unless otherwise stated, all root vegetables should be peeled prior to using.

The times given are an approximate guide only. Preparation times differ according to the techniques used by different people and the cooking times may also vary from those given.

Please note that any ingredients stated as being optional are not included in the nutritional values provided. The nutritional values given are approximate and provided as only a guide; they do not account for individual cooks, measuring skills, and portion sizes. The nutritional values provided are per serving or per item.

While the publisher of the book and the original author(s) of the recipes and other text have made all reasonable efforts to ensure that the information contained in this book is accurate and up to date at the time of publication, anyone reading this book should note the following important points:

Medical and pharmaceutical knowledge is constantly changing and the author(s) and the publisher cannot and do not guarantee the accuracy or appropriateness of the contents of this book.

In any event, this book is not intended to be, and should not be relied upon, as a substitute for appropriate, tailored professional advice. Both the author(s) and the publisher strongly recommend that a physician or other healthcare professional is consulted before embarking on major dietary changes.

For the reasons set out above, and to the fullest extent permitted by law, the author(s) and publisher: (i) cannot and do not accept any legal duty of care or responsibility in relation to the accuracy or appropriateness of the contents of this book, even where expressed as "advice" or using other words to this effect; and (ii) disclaim any liability, loss, damage, or risk that may be claimed or incurred as a consequence—directly or indirectly—of the use and/or application of any of the contents of this book.

JUICE

Nutritionists can often disagree, but there is one subject where there is no argument—that most of us don't eat enough fruit and vegetables. Getting your daily dose of vitamins and other nutrients from natural sources, such as fruit and vegetables, is a much better idea than relying on expensive dietary supplements; not only do they taste better, but nutritionists believe that fruit and vegetables contain a variety of other compounds, such as phytochemicals, that help us stay healthy and disease-free.

The benefits of eating a diet rich in fruit and vegetables is well-documented. It can reduce the risk of a whole host of medical conditions, including heart disease, stroke, certain types of cancer, cataracts, high blood pressure, dementia, and Alzheimer's disease. However, the benefits don't end there. Studies show that people who eat plenty of fruit and vegetables have fewer wrinkles and skin that looks more youthful.

The U.S. government recommends adults have 2 cups of fruit (but ½ cup of dried fruit counts as 1 cup, as does 1 cup of 100 percent fruit juice) daily plus 2½ cups of vegetables if you are female or 3 cups for males, but few of us—even people who love eating fruit and vegetable—manage to reach the target. Juices and smoothies offer the perfect solution. They are quick and easy to make and the whole family will love them.

Drink your Way
to *Health*
& Vitality

Juices such as Vegetable Belly Treat are a great way to disguise vegetables, so even the most reluctant vegetable eater can enjoy them. Variety may be the spice of life, but it's also a vital ingredient in a healthy balanced diet and is particularly important when it comes to fruit and vegetables, because different fruit and vegetables contain different phytochemicals that work together to keep us healthy in different ways.

Juices and smoothies are a wonderful way to expand the variety of fruit and vegetables in your diet. In this book, you'll find juices, such as Beat the Morning Blues, that have been designed to boost energy and give you a healthy boost of good nutrition to start the day, plus others, such as Up the Anti and Green Goddess, that will help to nourish and boost your immunity system. Other chapters focus on drinks that will help soothe, hydrate, or detox your body. Whatever your reason for juicing or making a smoothie, this book provides plenty of options that are not just healthy but delicious, too.

Juices vs Smoothies

What's the Difference?

Although in many ways juices and smoothies are similar—both are quick and easy to make, truly delicious, and packed with vitamins and minerals—there are also important differences between the two.

Juices are made by squeezing the liquid from fruit and/or vegetables. Much of the fiber is left behind when you make juice, which means your body doesn't have to work so hard to digest juices and the nutrients are absorbed quickly into the blood stream.

Smoothies are made by blending fruit and/or vegetables with other ingredients, such as milk, yogurt, nuts, or fruit juice. If you want to avoid dairy, you can use dairy-free alternatives, such as rice, oat, soy, or almond milk.

What Equipment Do I Need?

If you plan to make both smoothies and juices, you'll need to buy two separate machines. For smoothies, you'll need a smoothie maker or blender, but to make juices, you'll need a juice extractor.

The most basic juicer you can buy is an electronic citrus press. They are compact and easy to clean, however, they will juice only citrus fruits. To juice other fruit and vegetables, you will need to buy a juice extractor.

Before you invest in a juicer, it is worth thinking about how serious you are about juicing, how often you plan to use your juicer, and where you will be storing it. If you have the space on your work surface and are serious about juicing, a masticating model is a good choice.

Masticating juicers crush the fruit and vegetables and then push the juice out through a mesh wire. They tend to be heavier and more expensive than centrifugal juicers, but they do produce a larger quantity of juice and retain more nutrients. If you want to juice wheatgrass, this is the type of juicer you will need, too.

Centrifugal juicers are usually smaller and lighter so easier to store, but they can be noisy. Fruit and vegetables are fed via a tube onto a fast spinning metal filter with grating teeth. The juice and the pulp are separated by centrifugal force. Centrifugal juicers spin fast, which can introduce more oxygen and heat into the juice, whereas masticating models are much gentler.

With juicers, you definitely get what you pay for, and if you're serious about juicing, it's worth investing in the most sophisticated machine you can afford. If you're planning to make large quantities of juice all at once, choose a model that ejects pulp into a separate compartment, so you won't have to keep stopping to empty out the pulp.

What Ingredients Can I Use?

You can use almost any raw fruits, vegetables, or herbs to make juice, and once the juice is made, you can add in extras, such as spirulina powder. When you make juice, the juice is separated from the fiber, but, of course, you can always add some of the pulp/fiber back into the juice before you drink it. Some juices, especially the green vegetables, can be an acquired taste, but apple, carrot, red bell pepper, and citrus fruits are usually an instant success.

Try to use fruit and vegetables that are in season. Choose ripe but not overripe fruit, avoid bruised or wilted produce, and buy organic, if possible. Using a variety of different fruit and vegetables, or combining one or two in the same juice, will help you to make sure that you get the full range of nutrients.

Smoothies offer more versatility and, in fact, the possibilities are endless. You can use fresh, frozen, canned, or dried fruit or vegetables and blend them with milk, yogurt, dairy-free milk alternatives, nuts and seeds, nut butters, and protein powders.

Frozen and canned fruit in smoothies make a good alternative to fresh fruit, especially in the winter months when fresh fruit can be more expensive. Using frozen fruit gives smoothies a thick creamy consistency and helps them stay cold for longer, which is useful if you will not be drinking them immediately.

Dried fruits, such as apricots, prunes, and dates, can also be used to make smoothies. To make the dried fruit soft enough to puree, you'll need to soak them in fruit juice overnight. Levels of vitamins and some phytochemicals diminish during storage, so to minimize these losses, you should buy dried fruit little and often.

Give Me Some Hints & Tips!

- Prepare fruit and vegetables just before juicing. Wash thoroughly, scrubbing tough skinned varieties with a soft brush before juicing.

- Make sure all your fruit and vegetables are chopped as necessary into similar sizes; soft fruit, such as bananas, can be in larger chunks, while hard items, such as carrots, should be chopped small. Always use the provided plunger for feeding items into a juicer. Don't try to blend without adding liquid; put solids into a blender bowl and add liquid.

- It's always best to drink freshly prepared juice. Even when it's stored in the refrigerator, it can turn brown, which shows the nutrients are oxidizing. Cold-pressed juices tend to store well for longer (24 hours or more), if kept in the refrigerator.

- You can boost the nutritional value of juices and smoothies by adding other ingredients, such as chia seeds, wheat germ, nuts and seeds, or tahini. Try to avoid adding too much sugar.

- Keep any pantry supplements fresh. Pay attention to any expiration dates and discard out-of-date items. Store all items in a dry, dark, and preferably cool place in a sealed container. Always keep liquid supplements in the refrigerator.

- The pulp that remains when you've made the juice is a good source of fiber and contains vitamins and phytochemicals, so don't waste it. It can be used to thicken soup or in baking.

Whether it's to help you get the best start to the day, fuel you through a grueling workout, or just to avoid the afternoon slump at work, finding a healthy way to get a quick-and-easy energy boost is essential. These recipes are packed with energy-giving ingredients, and they are delicious, too. Try our Berry Jump-Start, Turbo Express, or Muesli Motivator.

ENERGY

Power Gulp

Serves: 1 | Prep: 10–15 minutes | Cook: none

Per serving : 471 CAL | 13.8G FAT | 1.2G SAT FAT | 85G CARBS | 63.4G SUGAR | 18.9G FIBER | 11.6G PROTEIN | 160MG SODIUM

Beets are a favorite vegetable among sportspeople. They are great for boosting stamina and making muscles work harder and are packed with vitamins, minerals, carbohydrates, protein, and powerful antioxidants.

Ingredients

2 beets, halved
3 tablespoons flaxseed
4 plums, quartered and pitted
1 cup seedless red grapes
1 cup chilled water
crushed ice, to serve (optional)

1. Feed the beets through a juicer.

2. Put the flaxseed into a blender and blend until finely ground. Add the beet juice, plums, grapes, and water and blend until smooth.

3. Pour into a glass, add crushed ice, if using, and serve immediately.

Single Shot Sports Boosters

Serves: 1 | Prep: 20 minutes | Cook: none

Have one of these potent juices just before you start strenuous exercise for a vitamin and mineral boost to energize muscles and aid performance. Prepare the boosters in advance and take to the gym in a well-sealed insulated thermos.

Per serving: 86 CAL | 0.3G FAT | TRACE SAT FAT | 19.1G CARBS | 13.5G SUGAR | 5.6G FIBER | 3.2G PROTEIN | 160MG SODIUM

Beet Booster

2 beets, halved

¼ cup chilled water (optional)

1. To make the beets booster, feed the beets through a juicer. Pour into a glass, top up with the water, if using, and serve.

Per serving: 84 CAL | 0.7G FAT | TRACE SAT FAT | 20.2G CARBS | 12.4G SUGAR | 4.1G FIBER | 1.6G PROTEIN | TRACE SODIUM

Kiwi Booster

2 kiwis, peeled
and coarsely chopped

1. To make the kiwi booster, feed the kiwis through a juicer. Pour into a glass and serve.

Per serving: 86 CAL | 0.5G FAT | TRACE SAT FAT | 21.7G CARBS | 14.9G SUGAR | 3.6G FIBER | 1.1G PROTEIN | TRACE SODIUM

Blueberry Booster

1 cup blueberries

¼ cup chilled water

1. To make the blueberry booster, put the blueberries and water into a blender and blend until smooth. Pour into a glass and serve.

Beet Booster

Kiwi Booster

Blueberry Booster

Sweet Beets

Beets have one of the highest sugar levels of any vegetable, with the equivalent of 1 teaspoon of natural fruit sugar in each 4-ounce serving, so it gives a great energy boost. It also contains folates, vitamin C, and potassium, which help regulate blood pressure and nerve function.

Tropical Watermelon Wonder

Serves: 2 | Prep: 15 minutes | Cook: none

Per serving: 528 CAL | 39.7G FAT | 34.7G SAT FAT | 47.5G CARBS | 26.3G SUGAR | 6G FIBER | 6.5G PROTEIN | TRACE SODIUM

Delicious watermelon is the ultimate in thirst-quenching fruits. Blending it with the tropical flavors of banana and coconut cream (not the sweetened cream of coconut) will give you a refreshingly exotic-tasting energy boost after a workout.

Ingredients

⅛ watermelon, peeled, seeded, and coarsely chopped

2 small bananas, peeled and coarsely chopped

1 cup coconut cream (available in larger supermarkets and Asian grocery stores) or coconut milk

1. Put the watermelon, bananas, and coconut cream or milk into a blender and process until combined.

2. Pour into chilled glasses and serve.

Red Pep-Up

Serves: 1 | Prep: 15 minutes | Cook: none

Per serving: 93 CAL | 0.5G FAT | TRACE SAT FAT | 21.9G CARBS | 10.9G SUGAR | 1.5G FIBER | 2.6G PROTEIN | 80MG SODIUM

Full of disease-fighting, antiaging antioxidants, this drink provides plenty of energy from its natural sweetness to help you get through the day.

Ingredients

2 fennel bulbs with leaves, halved
1 apple, halved
1 small red bell pepper, halved
1 carrot, halved

1. Remove a few leaves from the fennel and reserve.

2. Feed the apple, then the fennel and red bell pepper, then the carrot through a juicer.

3. Pour into a glass, garnish with the reserved fennel leaves, and serve.

Why Not Try?

Agave syrup and brown rice syrup can be used instead of honey. Agave syrup is naturally sweeter than honey. Brown rice syrup has a mild caramel flavor and is similar to maple syrup.

Berry Jump-Start

Serves: 1 | Prep: 10–15 minutes | Cook: none

Per serving : 288 CAL | 5.6G FAT | 3.1G SAT FAT | 57.9G CARBS | 40.5G SUGAR | 9.5G FIBER | 6.9G PROTEIN | 40MG SODIUM

This energizing, gorgeous-looking smoothie is chock-full of fresh berries and is a delicious and healthy way to jump-start your day.

Ingredients

1¼ cups blueberries
⅔ cup cranberries
⅔ cup plain yogurt
2 teaspoons honey
¼ cup chilled water

1. Put the blueberries and cranberries into a blender and blend.

2. Add the yogurt, honey, and water and blend again until smooth.

3. Pour into a glass and serve.

Blueberry Blast

Serves: 1 | Prep: 10–15 minutes | Cook: none

Per serving : 346 CAL | 8.2G FAT | 4G SAT FAT | 62.4G CARBS | 37G SUGAR | 6.8G FIBER | 12.1G PROTEIN | 80MG SODIUM

The blueberry is a superhero in the food world. When mixed with pear, plain yogurt, and chilled water, it will get you through the most hectic of schedules. You can use two apples instead of the water; just juice them with the pear.

Ingredients

1 pear, halved
¾ cup blueberries
¾ cup plain yogurt
3 tablespoons wheat germ
¾ cup chilled water
small handful of crushed ice
(optional)

1. Feed the pear through a juicer.

2. Pour the juice into a blender, add the blueberries, yogurt, wheat germ, and water, and blend until smooth. Add the crushed ice, if using, and blend again until smooth.

3. Pour into a glass and serve immediately.

Blueberries: Good Mood Food

The antioxidant power of blueberries has been shown to help stabilize brain function and protect the neural tissue from oxidative stress, which may improve memory and learning and reduce symptoms of depression.

Fennel

The European plant fennel is a valuable source of vitamin B6, playing a vital part in energy metabolism. It aids the breakdown of carbohydrates and proteins into glucose and amino acids, used for energy in the body. It also has a positive impact on skin and hair health, and it decreases the risks of heart disease and diabetes.

Pink Energy

Serves: 1 | Prep: 15–20 minutes | Cook: none

Per serving: 294 CAL | 5.2G FAT | 0.9G SAT FAT | 56.8G CARBS | 35.9G SUGAR | 10.1G FIBER | 10.5G PROTEIN | 40MG SODIUM

Ingredients

½ papaya, peeled, seeded, and coarsely chopped

1 cup hulled strawberries

1 banana, peeled and coarsely chopped

juice of ½ lime

1 cup unsweetened rice, almond, or soy milk

small handful of crushed ice (optional)

1. Put the papaya, strawberries, and banana into a blender and blend until smooth.

2. Add the lime juice and milk and blend again. Add the crushed ice, if using, and blend again until smooth.

3. Pour into a glass and serve.

Turbo Express

Serves: 1 | Prep: 15–20 minutes | Cook: none

Per serving: 338 CAL | 3.4G FAT | 0.7G SAT FAT | 76.2G CARBS | 54.7G SUGAR | 8.4G FIBER | 8.1G PROTEIN | 40MG SODIUM

Ingredients

¼ honeydew melon, seeded, peeled, and coarsely chopped

1 banana, peeled and coarsely chopped

1 kiwi, peeled and coarsely chopped

¾ cup seedless green grapes

small handful of watercress (optional)

½ cup unsweetened rice, almond, or soy milk

small handful of crushed ice (optional)

1. Put the melon, banana, kiwi, grapes, and watercress, if using, into a blender and blend well until smooth.

2. Add the milk and crushed ice, if using, and blend again until smooth.

3. Pour into a glass and serve immediately.

Juicing Oranges

Oranges vary greatly in the amount
of juice that they produce. If they
are kept at room temperature,
they will be easier to squeeze.
Adjust the thickness of this juice
with water as needed.

Raspberry Rejuvenator

Serves: 1 | Prep: 15 minutes | Cook: none

Per serving: 348 CAL | 3.1G FAT | 0.1G SAT FAT | 80.4G CARBS | 54.2G SUGAR | 13.5G FIBER | 4.6G PROTEIN | TRACE SODIUM

Raspberries and bananas are a delicious combination. They give the body a slowly released energy boost to reenergize you in a sustained way.

Ingredients

¼ cup goji berries

1 small banana, peeled and coarsely chopped

1 cup raspberries

juice of 2 oranges

small handful of crushed ice (optional)

chilled water, to taste

1. Put the goji berries into a blender and blend until finely ground.

2. Add the banana, raspberries, and orange juice and blend until smooth. Add the crushed ice, if using, and blend again until smooth.

3. Add water to taste, pour into a glass, and serve immediately.

Peach Energizer

Serves: 1 | Prep: 15–20 minutes | Cook: none

Per serving: 266 CAL | 8.9G FAT | 1.1G SAT FAT | 46.8G CARBS | 35.6G SUGAR | 4.7G FIBER | 5.4G PROTEIN | 40MG SODIUM

The grapefruit blast in this drink will perk you up and sharpen your senses, while the peach will provide natural sugars to boost your energy levels and the ginger will soothe and comfort.

Ingredients

1 pink or ruby grapefruit, rind and
a little pith removed, halved

1 carrot, halved

½-inch piece fresh ginger, peeled

1 large peach, pitted and
coarsely chopped

1 tablespoon light tahini

½ cup chilled water (optional)

small handful of crushed ice

1. Feed the grapefruit, then the carrot and ginger, through a juicer.

2. Pour the juice into a blender, add the peach, tahini, water, if using, and crushed ice and blend until smooth.

3. Pour into a glass and serve immediately.

Vegan Power Shake

Serves: 2 | Prep: 10–15 minutes | Cook: none

Per serving : 245 CAL | 16.9G FAT | 2.1G SAT FAT | 18.1G CARBS | 10.4G SUGAR | 2.8G FIBER | 6.5G PROTEIN | TRACE SODIUM

This is a great milk shake for anyone who is vegan or lactose intolerant. Banana and maple syrup blend with the milk to make a deliciously creamy, potassium-rich shake.

Ingredients

1 large banana, peeled and coarsely chopped

1½ cups chilled soy milk

2 tablespoons vegan omega 3-6-9 oil

1 teaspoon maple syrup

1. Put the banana into a blender with the milk and omega oil.

2. Blend gently until thoroughly combined. Add maple syrup to taste.

3. Serve immediately in tall drinking glasses.

Bountiful Bananas

Naturally rich in fruit sugar and starch, bananas are great energy-boosting foods and have a high amount of potassium. They can help regulate blood pressure and may reduce the risk of heart attacks, strokes, and cancer.

Muesli Motivator

Serves: 1 | Prep: 15 minutes | Cook: none

Per serving: 450 CAL | 18.5G FAT | 1.4G SAT FAT | 65.1G CARBS | 31.5G SUGAR | 16.6G FIBER | 12.8G PROTEIN | TRACE SODIUM

Refreshing and extra-zingy, this smoothie makes a delicious energy-packed breakfast. The natural fruit sugars and slow-release complex carbs from the grapefruit pith, oats, and almonds will keep you feeling full until lunchtime.

Ingredients

¼ cup rolled oats

⅓ cup slivered almonds

½ ruby red grapefruit, rind and a little pith removed, seeded and coarsely chopped

1¼ cups raspberries

juice of 2 oranges

⅓ cup chilled water

1. Put the oats and almonds into a blender and blend until finely ground.

2. Add the grapefruit, raspberries, orange juice, and water and blend until smooth.

3. Pour into a glass and serve.

Make It Perfect

Be sure to cut grapefruit into small
pieces before putting it in the blender
so that you get a smooth juice.

Almond Butter & Raspberry Bliss

Serves: 2 | Prep: 10 minutes | Cook: none

Per serving : 338CAL | 14.1G FAT | 1G SAT FAT | 28.4G CARBS | 11.6G SUGAR | 10.7G FIBER | 6.7G PROTEIN | 80MG SODIUM

If you don't usually eat breakfast, try this smoothie. It is a really quick, tasty, and nutrient-packed start to a busy day.

Ingredients

1 banana, peeled and coarsely chopped
1⅔ cups raspberries
1⅔ cups unsweetened almond milk
2½ tablespoons almond butter
4 teaspoons stevia granules
2 teaspoons vanilla extract
ice cubes

1. Put the banana into a blender with the raspberries.

2. Add the almond milk, almond butter, stevia granules, and vanilla extract. Top up with ice cubes.

3. Blend until smooth. Drink immediately or chill overnight.

Mango for Energy

A mango is 14 percent natural sugar, and it can be quickly converted into energy by the body. It is also rich in beta-carotene and vitamin C.

Tropical Energizer

Serves: 1 | Prep: 15–20 minutes | Cook: none

Per serving : 394 CAL | 6.7G FAT | 0.9G SAT FAT | 70.4G CARBS | 47.5G SUGAR | 9.1G FIBER | 7.6G PROTEIN | TRACE SODIUM

Papaya and mango are both rich in natural fruit sugars, which give an energy boost. They're also easy to digest and gentle on the stomach.

Ingredients

1 banana, peeled and coarsely chopped

½ papaya, peeled, seeded, and coarsely chopped

½ mango, pitted, peeled, and coarsely chopped

juice of 1 lime

¾-inch piece fresh ginger, peeled and finely grated

2 teaspoons hemp oil

½ cup unsweetened rice, almond, or soy milk

small handful of crushed ice

1. Put the chopped banana, papaya, and mango into a blender and blend until smooth.

2. Add the lime, ginger, oil, milk, and crushed ice and blend again.

3. Pour into a glass and serve immediately.

Almonds

Almonds are rich in healthy monounsaturated fatty acids, the good kind of fat that contributes to increased heart health and lower cholesterol levels. The slow digestive process of almonds and their stack of nutrients, such as biotin and manganese, produce a more sustained type of energy in the body, leaving you feeling fuller and more alert for a longer period of time.

Banana Breakfast Wake-Up

Serves: 2 | Prep: 5 minutes | Cook: none

Per serving : 259 CAL | 3.8G FAT | 0.7G SAT FAT | 55.7G CARBS | 34.4G SUGAR | 6G FIBER | 8.3G PROTEIN | TRACE SODIUM

A speedy, sustaining breakfast-in-a-glass, this delicious shake is perfect for those days when time is short and you need long-lasting energy.

Ingredients

2 large ripe bananas, peeled and coarsely chopped

2 tablespoons oat bran

2 tablespoons honey

1 tablespoon lemon juice

1¼ cups soy milk

ground cinnamon, to serve (optional)

1. Put all the ingredients into a blender and blend until smooth.

2. Pour into tall glasses, sprinkle with ground cinnamon, if using, and serve immediately.

Honey Goodness

Honey supplies energy in the form of simple carbohydrates and is a mixture of fructose and glucose. The clearer the honey, the higher the level of fructose. Sweet foods stimulate the brain to produce endorphins, the body's natural pain-killers.

Strawberry & Vanilla Delight

Serves: 2 | Prep: 10–15 minutes | Cook: none

Per serving : 151 CAL | 2.8G FAT | 0.3G SAT FAT | 24.6G CARBS | 16.7G SUGAR | 0.8G FIBER | 4.7G PROTEIN | TRACE SODIUM

This creamy soy shake makes a great quick breakfast, or you could drink it as an instant energy boost at any time of day. Replace the soy milk with unsweetened almond milk for a subtle difference in flavor.

Ingredients

1⅓ cups halved, hulled strawberries

1 cup plain soy yogurt

⅓ cup chilled soy milk

2 teaspoons vanilla extract

1. Put the strawberry halves, yogurt, milk, and vanilla extract into a blender and gently blend until thoroughly combined.

2. Serve immediately in tall drinking glasses.

Raw Cacao Milk Shake

Serves: 4 | Prep: 10 minutes | Cook: none

Per serving: 198 CAL | 10.8G FAT | 2G SAT FAT | 24.9G CARBS | 15.5G SUGAR | 3.9G FIBER | 5.2G PROTEIN | 40MG SODIUM

Great for waking up your taste buds first thing, or for a nutritious chocolate hit at any time, this delicious dairy-free and gluten-free milk shake provides a perfect pick-me-up that is suitable for vegetarians and vegans, too.

Ingredients

1⅔ cups almond milk
⅔ cup dried dates
⅔ cup cashew nuts
2 tablespoons raw cacao powder
1 teaspoon ground cinnamon
handful of ice cubes
1 tablespoon orange zest, to decorate

1. Put the almond milk, dates, nuts, cacao powder, cinnamon, and ice into a blender.

2. Blend thoroughly until the milk shake has a thick pouring consistency.

3. Pour into chilled glasses, decorate with the orange zest, and serve.

Raw Cacao

Raw cacao is naturally high in antioxidants, magnesium, iron, and fiber. It helps protect the nervous system and lowers blood pressure and it can also aid in reducing the risk of nerve damage, cardiovascular disease, diabetes, and stroke.

Blueberry Thrill

Serves: 2 | Prep: 10 minutes | Cook: none

Per serving : 85 CAL | 2.7G FAT | 1.8G SAT FAT | 11.3G CARBS | 8.3G SUGAR | 1.3G FIBER | 5G PROTEIN | TRACE SODIUM

Blueberries have long been regarded as one of nature's superfoods, and they're delicious, too. The blueberry season is short, but this easy smoothie uses frozen blueberries that are available all year round.

Ingredients

½ cup Greek-style yogurt

½ cup water

1 cup frozen blueberries

2 whole frozen blueberries, to decorate

1. Put the yogurt, water, and blueberries into a blender and blend until smooth.

2. Pour into glasses, top each with a whole frozen blueberry, and serve.

We've compiled our favorite thirst-quenching drinks that are not only rehydrating but are also made from totally natural and nutritious ingredients. For hot summer days, post-exercise cooldowns, or any time you want a refreshing juice, turn to recipes in this chapter, such as our Summer Corn Quencher, Citrus Cleanser, Lettuce Elixir, or Kale Green Tropic.

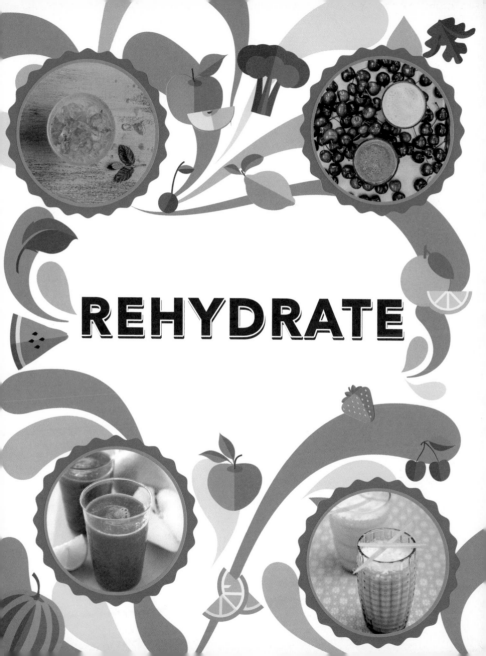

REHYDRATE

How to Juice Herbs

To get the most juice from herbs, sandwich them between firmer fruit or vegetables so that their weight helps to press down on the leaves as they go through the juicer chute.

Tantalizing Tomato Refresher

Serves: 1 | Prep: 10–15 minutes | Cook: none

Per serving : 126 CAL | 1G FAT | 0.1G SAT FAT | 27.5G CARBS | 15.7G SUGAR | 2G FIBER | 5.2G PROTEIN | 120MG SODIUM

The success of this refreshing juice depends on the quality of the tomatoes; homegrown and just-picked ones are perfect, but otherwise choose tomatoes of a generous size and with a deep color that are still on the vine for the best flavor.

Ingredients

2 carrots, halved

small handful of fresh basil leaves

1 celery stalk, halved

1-inch slice of broccoli stem

4 tomatoes

small handful of crushed ice (optional)

1. Feed the carrots, then most of the basil, the celery, broccoli, and tomatoes through a juicer.

2. Fill a glass halfway with crushed ice, if using, then pour in the juice.

3. Garnish with the remaining basil leaves and serve immediately.

Cool as a Cucumber

Serves: 1 | Prep: 10–15 minutes | Cook: none

Per serving : 153 CAL | 0.9G FAT | 0.2G SAT FAT | 37.3G CARBS | 25.7G SUGAR | 1.8G FIBER | 3.6G PROTEIN | 40MG SODIUM

This is like a cooling summer salad in a glass: light and fresh, with a gentle pepperiness from the arugula, a dash of mouth-freshening garden mint, and a hint of sweetness from the apple.

Ingredients

½ cucumber, halved

⅓ cup arugula

3 fresh mint sprigs

1 zucchini

1 celery stalk, halved

1 apple, halved

small handful of crushed ice (optional)

1 fresh mint sprig, to garnish

1. Feed the cucumber, arugula, and mint through a juicer, followed by the zucchini, celery, and apple.

2. Fill a glass halfway with crushed ice, if using, then pour in the juice and serve immediately, garnished with a mint sprig.

Not Fond of Celery?

Omit it and add a little more cucumber instead.

Celery & Apple Revitalizer

Serves: 2 | Prep: 10–15 minutes | Cook: none

Per serving : 235 CAL | 9.9G FAT | 5.6G SAT FAT | 27.5G CARBS | 25.2G SUGAR | 2G FIBER | 10.1G PROTEIN | 160MG SODIUM

This milk shake will do you good. Celery and apple are the perfect combination in this beverage, which is great on hot summer days. Serve it in tall glasses with strips of celery to decorate.

Ingredients

3 celery stalks, chopped
1 apple, peeled, cored, and diced
2¾ cups milk
pinch of sugar
salt (optional)
4 strips of celery, to garnish

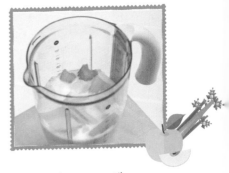

1. Put the celery, apple, and milk into a blender and process until thoroughly combined.

2. Stir in the sugar and some salt, if using.

3. Pour into chilled glasses, decorate with strips of celery, and serve.

Orange Refresher

Serves: 1 | Prep: 10–15 minutes | Cook: none

Per serving: 131 CAL | 0.6G FAT | 0.1G SAT FAT | 31.8G CARBS | 27.9G SUGAR | 5G FIBER | 2.9G PROTEIN | 40MG SODIUM

A glass of freshly squeezed orange juice doesn't just have to be limited to breakfast. With the addition of fresh mint and lusciously sweet melon, this rehydrating juice will refresh you at any time of the day.

Ingredients

1 orange, rind and a little pith removed, halved

1 large fresh mint sprig

½ small cantaloupe, peeled, seeded, and coarsely chopped

1–2 fresh mint sprigs, to decorate

1. Put the orange into a food processor or blender with the mint and melon and process until smooth.

2. Pour into a glass and serve decorated with mint sprigs.

Summer Corn Quencher

Serves: 1 | Prep: 15 minutes | Cook: none

Per serving : 222 CAL | 2.1G FAT | 0.3G SAT FAT | 51.7G CARBS | 30.4G SUGAR | 2.3G FIBER | 5.2G PROTEIN | TRACE SODIUM

Ingredients

1 fresh ear of corn, shucked

4 fresh cilantro sprigs

1 yellow bell pepper, seeded and halved

1 apple, halved

small handful of crushed ice (optional)

1. Cut the kernels from the corn, then feed them through a juicer.

2. Feed the cilantro, followed by the yellow bell pepper and then the apple, through the juicer.

3. Fill a glass halfway with crushed ice, if using, then pour in the juice and serve immediately.

Cherry Aid

Serves: 1 | Prep: 20 minutes | Cook: none

Per serving : 376 CAL | 4.8G FAT | 0.6G SAT FAT | 87.7G CARBS | 57.1G SUGAR | 4.8G FIBER | 5.2G PROTEIN | TRACE SODIUM

Ingredients

2 pears, halved

1 tablespoon chia seeds

1 cup pitted cherries

½ cup chilled water

small handful of crushed ice (optional)

1. Feed the pears through a juicer.

2. Put the chia seeds into a blender and blend until finely ground. Add the pear juice, cherries, water, and crushed ice, if using, and blend until smooth.

3. Pour into a glass and serve immediately.

Melon, Pear & Ginger Spritzer

Serves: 1 | Prep: 15–20 minutes | Cook: none

Per serving: 247 CAL | 0.8G FAT | 0.2G SAT FAT | 63.9G CARBS | 49.8G SUGAR | 2.2G FIBER | 2.8G PROTEIN | 80MG SODIUM

Here is a refreshingly healthy version of ginger beer, with no chemicals and no added sugars—just 100 percent natural ingredients.

Ingredients

½ honeydew melon, thickly sliced and peeled

½-inch piece fresh ginger, peeled

1 pear, halved

small handful of crushed ice (optional)

½ cup sparkling mineral water, chilled

1. Feed the melon, followed by the ginger and then the pear, through a juicer.

2. Fill a glass halfway with crushed ice, if using, then pour in the juice.

3. Top up with the mineral water and serve immediately.

Water vs. Juices

When you exercise, you lose many of the minerals in your body through sweat. Water alone will rehydrate you, but so can juices. Homemade fruit and vegetable juices also boost your energy and vitamin and mineral intake and help you rehydrate more quickly, speeding up recovery time. A mixture of the two in a homemade isotonic sports drink is best.

Celery

Celery is sometimes referred to as "crunchy water," because of its incredible hydrating properties. Rich in minerals, just a few celery stalks can replenish levels of sodium, iron, and zinc in the body. Because it aids the body's natural composition, it is more effective in hydration than water alone, which is the reason why it's also so beneficial in keeping your digestive system clear.

Kale Green Tropic

Serves: 1 | Prep: 10–15 minutes | Cook: none

Per serving : 53 CAL | 0.3G FAT | TRACE SAT FAT | 12.2G CARBS | 7.7G SUGAR | 2.2G FIBER | 1.7G PROTEIN | TRACE SODIUM

Full of fresh pineapple flavor, this delicious green shot is boosted with the B vitamins and essential minerals and will give you an immediate lift.

Ingredients

¼ cup shredded kale

⅓ cup peeled and coarsely chopped pineapple

½ cup spinach

⅛ teaspoon wheatgrass powder

¼ cup chilled water

1 pineapple wedge, to garnish

1. Put the kale and the pineapple into a blender with the spinach and wheatgrass powder.

2. Pour the water over the top and blend until smooth.

3. Serve immediately, garnished with the pineapple wedge.

Wonderful
Wheatgrass

As you get used to the flavor of
wheatgrass, increase the amount
to 1 teaspoon.

Red Pepper Reviver

Serves: 1 | Prep: 10–15 minutes | Cook: none

Per serving : 100 CAL | 10.0G FAT | 1.0G SAT FAT | 10.0G CARBS | 5.0G SUGAR | 1.0G FIBER | 1.0G PROTEIN | TRACE SODIUM

This zingy juice is sure to wake you up if you're having a midmorning snooze. Black pepper is an unexpectedly fiery spice—handle it with care.

Ingredients

2 carrots, halved

2 tomatoes, halved

1 large red bell pepper, seeded and halved

2 teaspoons lemon juice

pinch of pepper, plus extra to garnish (optional)

4–6 strips of shredded carrot, to garnish

1. Feed the carrots, followed by the tomatoes and then the red bell pepper, through a juicer.

2. Stir in the lemon juice and pepper.

3. Pour into a glass, garnish with the strips of shredded carrot and pepper, if using, and serve.

Thumbs Up for Tomatoes

Tomatoes contain 90 percent water, so they are great for rehydration. They are rich in lycopene, a carotenoid pigment that turns them red. It is thought this may help prevent some forms of cancer. They are also a good source of potassium, with smaller amounts of vitamins C and E.

Citrus Cleanser

Serves: 1 | Prep: 15 minutes | Cook: none

Per serving : 288 CAL | 0.8G FAT | TRACE SAT FAT | 75G CARBS | 53.2G SUGAR | 3.3G FIBER | 3.8G PROTEIN | TRACE SODIUM

Citrus fruit can stimulate the digestive system. In traditional folk medicine, it was thought that they also acted as a cleanser and astringent, stimulating the liver and gallbladder to function properly.

Ingredients

1 pink or ruby grapefruit, rind and a little pith removed, halved

1 orange, rind and a little pith removed, halved

1 lime, rind and pith removed from half

1 large pear, halved

small handful of crushed ice (optional)

1. Feed the grapefruit, orange, lime, and then the pear through a juicer.

2. Fill a glass halfway with crushed ice, if using, then pour in the juice and serve immediately.

Grapefruit Nutrition

Grapefruit is a great source of vitamin C. It is also packed with flavonoids (natural chemical compounds that may reduce early damage to DNA and cell membranes).

Red Reviver

Serves: 1 | Prep: 10 minutes | Cook: none

Per serving: 200 CAL | 0.6G FAT | TRACE SAT FAT | 50.2G CARBS | 30.8G SUGAR | 11.6G FIBER | 3.8G PROTEIN | 160MG SODIUM

The naturally sweet flavor of this deliciously vibrant red pick-me-up could be overwhelming, but it is subtly cut with tangy lime and spicy ginger.

Ingredients

2 small beets, halved

1 carrot, halved

1 pear, halved

½ lime, rind and pith removed, seeded, and coarsely chopped

1-inch piece fresh ginger, peeled

1. Put the beets and carrot into a blender and blend until smooth.

2. Add the pear, lime, and ginger and blend again until smooth.

3. Pour into a glass and serve.

Lettuce Elixir

Serves: 1 | Prep: 10–15 minutes | Cook: none

Per serving : 157 CAL | 1.2G FAT | 0.1G SAT FAT | 35.8G CARBS | 23.6G SUGAR | 2.7G FIBER | 5G PROTEIN | 200MG SODIUM

Lettuce, celery, and apple all have a high water content, so they are useful in helping the body to flush out toxins. This cleansing drink also tastes delicious.

Ingredients

2 cups coarsely chopped romaine lettuce

4 celery stalks, coarsely chopped

1 green apple, halved

1 cup fresh flat-leaf parsley

1 teaspoon spirulina powder

1 romaine lettuce leaf, to garnish

crushed ice, to serve

1. Feed the lettuce, celery, and apple through a juicer with the parsley.

2. Stir through the spirulina powder until combined.

3. Pour the beverage over crushed ice, if using, and serve immediately, garnished with the lettuce leaf.

Raspberry & Watermelon Crush

Serves: 1 | Prep: 15–20 minutes | Cook: none

Per serving : 125 CAL | 1G FAT | TRACE SAT FAT | 30.6G CARBS | 17.8G SUGAR | 8.4G FIBER | 2.7G PROTEIN | TRACE SODIUM

As the name suggests, watermelon is packed full of water, so what better way to rehydrate your body than with this delicately flavored smoothie blended with the natural sweetness of raspberries and a hint of tangy lime?

Ingredients

¼ small watermelon, peeled, coarsely chopped, and most of the black seeds removed

½ lime, rind and most of the pith removed, seeded, and coarsely chopped

1 cup raspberries

small handful of crushed ice

1. Put the watermelon and lime into a blender and blend until smooth.

2. Add the raspberries and crushed ice and blend again.

3. Pour into a glass and serve immediately.

Cut Down on Caffeine

Most of us drink far too much caffeine-loaded coffee and tea. Instead of quenching your thirst, these can lead to dehydration and reduce your stimulus to drink. Start choosing healthy, rehydrating juices and you will see a difference. They not only boost fluid levels but offer a nutrient hit at the same time.

Pink Zinger

Serves: 1 | Prep: 10–15 minutes | Cook: none

Per serving : 166 CAL | 0.6G FAT | TRACE SAT FAT | 43.5G CARBS | 31.7G SUGAR | 8G FIBER | 3.5G PROTEIN | TRACE SODIUM

This pink citrus cleanser will tantalize your taste buds and get your digestive juices flowing efficiently. It's a delicious breakfast drink, but it would also make a great-tasting nonalcoholic aperitif before a big meal.

Ingredients

1 pink grapefruit, rind and a little pith removed, seeded, and coarsely chopped

1 orange, rind and a little pith removed, seeded, and coarsely chopped

½ lemon, rind and a little pith removed, seeded, and coarsely chopped

½ lime, rind and a little pith removed, seeded, and coarsely chopped

1–2 lime slices, to decorate

1. Put the grapefruit, orange, lemon, and lime into a blender and process until smooth.

2. Pour into glasses and decorate with the lime slices.

Cucumber

Staying hydrated is essential to bodily health and the high water content of cucumber contributes to this. Offering a little something extra than regular water, cucumber contains high levels of vitamin C, vitamin A, and an array of antioxidants, which help to keep your blood pressure down and your skin healthy.

Grapefruit Crush

Serves: 1 | Prep: 10–15 minutes | Cook: none

Per serving: 185 CAL | 1.2G FAT | 0.1G SAT FAT | 43.5G CARBS | 28.7G SUGAR | 3G FIBER | 4.7G PROTEIN | 160MG SODIUM

This fresh and cooling juice is mixed with coconut water, which is packed with electrolytes and minerals to help counter dehydration.

Ingredients

½ cucumber, coarsely chopped

½ pink grapefruit, rind and a little pith removed, seeded, and coarsely chopped

2 kiwis, peeled and coarsely chopped

2 celery stalks, coarsely chopped

1 teaspoon maca powder

¼ cup coconut water

1 pink grapefruit section, to garnish

crushed ice, to serve (optional)

1. Feed the cucumber, grapefruit, kiwis, and celery through a juicer.

2. Stir through the maca powder and coconut water until combined.

3. Pour over crushed ice, if using, garnish with a grapefruit section, and serve immediately.

Why Not Try?

Substitute a flavored coconut water, such as coconut water with passion fruit or açai.

Dark Beet Thirst Quencher

Serves: 1 | Prep: 10–15 minutes| Cook: none

Per serving : 126 CAL | 1.8G FAT | 0.9G SAT FAT | 26G CARBS | 21.1G SUGAR | 4.8G FIBER | 4.2G PROTEIN | 0.3G SALT

Cool down on a hot day with this gorgeous-looking thirst-quencher. The natural sweetness of the beets will make it surprisingly tempting for kids.

Ingredients

1 orange, seeded, and rind
and a little pith removed

2 cooked beets

3 tablespoons plain yogurt

⅓ cup chilled water

1. Remove a section from the orange, cut it in half, and reserve, then coarsely chop the remainder.

2. Put the beets and orange into a blender and blend until smooth. Add the yogurt and water and blend again.

3. Pour into a glass. Thread the reserved orange pieces through a toothpick, place across the top of the glass, and serve.

Stay Hydrated

Water makes up about 70 percent of our muscles and 75 percent of our brains. In everyday breathing we lose about 2 cups water, so it is important to keep the body hydrated all year round, not only just when the weather is hot.

Apple Cooler

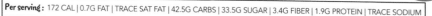

Serves: 2 | Prep: 15 minutes| Cook: none

Per serving : 172 CAL | 0.7G FAT | TRACE SAT FAT | 42.5G CARBS | 33.5G SUGAR | 3.4G FIBER | 1.9G PROTEIN | TRACE SODIUM

This delicious combination of fruits is given added tanginess with the addition of orange juice. Apples and strawberries are both naturally sweet, so be sure to taste the juice before adding any extra sugar.

Ingredients

2 apples, peeled and coarsely chopped

⅓ cup hulled strawberries

juice of 4 oranges

sugar (optional)

4 apple slices, to decorate

1. Put the apples, strawberries, and orange juice into a blender and process until smooth.

2. Taste and sweeten with sugar, if using.

3. Decorate with the apple slices and serve immediately.

With spirulina

Without spirulina

New to Spirulina?

Made from cultivated algae, spirulina contains chlorophyll, vitamin E, the B group of vitamins, linolenic acid, calcium, iron, protein, and zinc. Look for it in packages in health food stores.

Green Steam

Serves: 1 | Prep: 10–15 minutes | Cook: none

Per serving: 205 CAL | 1.4G FAT | 0.2G SAT FAT | 46.5G CARBS | 32.7G SUGAR | 2.1G FIBER | 6.7G PROTEIN | 80MG SODIUM

Because melon contains such a high proportion of water, it is great for rehydrating. The addition of spirulina, which contains blood-cleansing chlorophyll, makes this juice perfect for purifying the system.

Ingredients

1⅓ cups sugar snap peas

2-inch piece of cucumber

2 kiwis, peeled and coarsely chopped

¼ honeydew melon, peeled and thickly sliced

1 teaspoon spirulina powder (optional)

1 cup chilled water

small handful of crushed ice (optional)

1 cucumber stick, to serve

1. Feed the peas, cucumber, and kiwis through a juicer, followed by the melon slices.

2. Stir in the spirulina powder, if using, and top up with the water.

3. Fill a glass halfway with crushed ice, if using, then pour in the juice and serve immediately with a cucumber stick for a stirrer.

For times when you want to up your intake of vitamins, minerals, and "the good stuff," these healthy juices are the easy answer. Recipes such as our Vegetable Belly Treat, Spring Clean, Up the Anti, and Winter Pick-Me-Up are sure to help you on your way to feeling nourished and healthy. And the fact that they all taste and look delicious is just a bonus.

NOURISH

Crimson Vitality

Serves: 1 | Prep: 10–15 minutes | Cook: none

Per serving : 287 CAL | 0.9G FAT | 0.1G SAT FAT | 74.1G CARBS | 49.5G SUGAR | 3.9G FIBER | 3G PROTEIN | 80G SODIUM

Good health depends on every cell in the body receiving its fair share of nutrition. Your blood absorbs vital nutrition and circulates around the body. This vitality-boosting juice is an easy way for the body to digest vital vitamins and minerals.

Ingredients

1 beet, halved

1 cup cranberries

½-inch piece fresh ginger, peeled

2 apples, quartered

small handful of crushed ice (optional)

chilled water, to taste

1. Feed the beet, then the cranberries and ginger, followed by the apples, through a juicer.

2. Fill a glass halfway with crushed ice, if using, pour in the juice, top up with water to taste, and serve immediately.

Use the Beet Greens

If your beet has fresh, vibrant leaves instead of tired, limp-looking ones, add them to the juicer, too.

Muscular Magic

Serves: 1 | Prep: 15–20 minutes | Cook: none

Per serving : 530 CAL | 32.3G FAT | 3.4G SAT FAT | 59.1G CARBS | 27.8G SUGAR | 13.3G FIBER | 15.5G PROTEIN | 120MG SODIUM

Ingredients

1 cup green curly kale

small handful of fresh flat-leaf parsley

½ head of romaine lettuce

2 celery stalks, halved

1 apple, halved

½ lemon, rind and a little pith removed

⅓ cup slivered almonds

½ avocado, pitted, flesh scooped from the skin

small handful of crushed ice

1. Feed the kale, then the parsley and lettuce, followed by the celery, apple, and lemon, through a juicer.

2. Put the almonds into a blender and blend until finely ground. Add the kale juice mix and avocado flesh and blend again until smooth. Add the crushed ice and blend again until smooth.

3. Pour into a glass and serve immediately.

Natural Apple Booster

Serves: 1 | Prep: 10–15 minutes| Cook: none

Per serving : 386 CAL | 10G FAT | 1G SAT FAT | 81.7G CARBS | 62.5G SUGAR | 3.6G FIBER | 1.4G PROTEIN | TRACE SODIUM

Ingredients

3 apples, halved

2 teaspoons flaxseed oil

1 teaspoon honey

¼ teaspoon ground cinnamon

small handful of crushed ice (optional)

1 cinnamon stick (optional)

1. Feed the apples through a juicer. Stir in the oil, honey, and ground cinnamon.

2. Pour the juice into a blender, add the crushed ice, if using, and blend until smooth.

3. Pour into a glass and serve with the cinnamon stick as a stirrer, if using.

Kiwi Juice

Serves: 1 | Prep: 10 minutes | Cook: none

Per serving : 216 CAL | 0.9G FAT | 0.1G SAT FAT | 56G CARBS | 42.9G SUGAR | 7.5G FIBER | 2.1G PROTEIN | TRACE SODIUM

Kiwi is loaded with vitamin C, each fruit providing more of this protective vitamin than that traditional source of the orange. Green grapes, apples, and kiwis are all high in fiber, so do your digestion a favor with this delicious juice.

Ingredients

1 kiwi, peeled and coarsely chopped

1 apple, halved

¾ cup seedless green grapes

crushed ice, to serve (optional)

1. Put the kiwi and apple into a blender and blend until smooth.

2. Add the grapes and process again.

3. Pour into a glass and serve, or pour over crushed ice, if using.

Cranberry & Pineapple Fatigue Buster

Serves: 1 | Prep: 15 minutes | Cook: none

Per serving : 324 CAL | 9.6G FAT | 1G SAT FAT | 59.2G CARBS | 29.5G SUGAR | 17.9G FIBER | 6.8G PROTEIN | TRACE SODIUM

This fruit combination works well, with the natural sweetness of the pineapple balancing the sharpness of the cranberries. Take it to a training session in a thermos to give a boost to valuable glycogen stores before and after a workout.

Ingredients

2 tablespoons chia seeds

⅓ small pineapple, peeled and coarsely chopped

1 cup cranberries

small handful of crushed ice (optional)

1. Put the chia seeds into a blender and blend until finely ground.

2. Add the pineapple and cranberries and blend until smooth.

3. Fill a glass halfway with crushed ice, if using, then pour in the juice and serve immediately.

Soothing Pineapple

Rich in energy-boosting fruit sugars and vitamin C, pineapple also contains the digestive enzyme bromelain, which can have a calming effect on the stomach and so help anyone who feels nauseous after a strenuous workout or marathon run.

Vegetable Belly Treat

Serves: 1 | Prep: 15–20 minutes | Cook: none

Per serving : 302 CAL | 10.5G FAT | 1.4G SAT FAT | 50.3G CARBS | 37.1G SUGAR | 8G FIBER | 5.8G PROTEIN | 40MG SODIUM

Wake up your body and stimulate your digestive system with this fresh-tasting orange and tomato drink. The chile delivers a real kick, so those taste buds will definitely be shaken up.

Ingredients

3 oranges, rind and a little pith removed

1 carrot, halved

2 tomatoes, coarsely chopped

⅓ cup chilled water

1 small green chile, halved

2 celery stalks, thickly sliced

2 teaspoons hempseed oil

1. Cut 2 oranges in half and feed through a juicer with the carrot. Pour the juice into a blender.

2. Coarsely chop and seed the remaining orange, then put it into the blender with the tomatoes and water and blend until smooth. Add the chile and celery and blend again until smooth.

3. Pour into a glass, stir in the oil, and serve.

Hurrah for Hempseed Oil

Hempseed oil contains a good balance of both omega-3 and omega-6 fats. Scientists have found that it is the balance of these fats that is important in maintaining health and protecting us from disease.

Supergreens

Serves: 1 | Prep: 15–20 minutes | Cook: none

Per serving : 323 CAL | 18.7G FAT | 2.9G SAT FAT | 41.7G CARBS | 20G SUGAR | 10G FIBER | 5.7G PROTEIN | 40MG SODIUM

**This superb smoothie is packed with antioxidants, vitamins, and minerals.
The spirulina is also a great protein booster.**

Ingredients

1 pear, halved

1½ cups young spinach

4 fresh flat-leaf parsley sprigs

¼ cucumber, coarsely chopped

½ avocado, pitted, flesh
scooped from the skin

½ teaspoon spirulina powder

chilled water, to taste

1 Brazil nut, coarsely chopped

1. Feed the pear through a juicer. Pour the juice into a blender, add the spinach, parsley, cucumber, and avocado, and blend until smooth. Pour into a glass.

2. Mix the spirulina with just enough water to make a thick liquid, then swirl this into the juice.

3. Sprinkle with the chopped Brazil nut and serve.

Apricot Buzz

Serves: 2 | Prep 10–15 minutes | Cook: none

Per serving : 86 CAL | 0.5G FAT | TRACE SAT FAT | 20.4G CARBS | 15.8G SUGAR | 4.2G FIBER | 2.1G PROTEIN | TRACE SODIUM

When apricots are ripe and bursting with flavor, this nutritious juice will go down especially well. Serve with ice on a warm summer morning.

Ingredients

6 apricots, pitted

1 orange, rind and a little pith removed, seeded, and coarsely chopped

1 fresh lemongrass stalk, coarsely chopped

¾-inch piece fresh ginger, peeled

ice cubes, to serve

1. Put the apricots, orange, lemongrass, and ginger into a blender and blend until combined.

2. Pour the mixture into glasses, add ice, and serve.

Cinnamon

Cinnamon contains anti-inflammatory properties and also has the ability to stabilize blood sugar levels, a function of particular interest to people with diabetes. Its spiciness has a curative impact on the common cold and respiratory infections, and its warming quality almost makes the internal nourishment it provides something tangible.

Say Yes to Soy

Adding soy yogurt or soy milk to
a juice is a great way to boost its
protein levels. Choose soy yogurt or
milk that is unsweetened.

Cherry Pink

Serves: 1 | Prep: 20–25 minutes | Cook: none

Per serving : 389 CAL | 1.8G FAT | 0.2G SAT FAT | 98.6G CARBS | 75.6G SUGAR | 12.7G FIBER | 5.7G PROTEIN | TRACE SODIUM

This creamy drink is made with soy yogurt, which boosts its calcium content and is suitable for vegans and vegetarians. Delicious grapes and cherries provide an antioxidant boost, and the sweet flavors are rounded out with the tang of lime.

Ingredients

2⅓ cups pitted dark sweet cherries

1 apple, halved

½ lime, rind and pith removed, seeded, and coarsely chopped

⅔ cup red grapes

3 tablespoons soy yogurt

1. Put the cherries, apple, lime, and grapes into a blender and blend until smooth. Whisk in the yogurt.

2. Pour into a glass and serve.

Spring Clean

Serves: 1 | Prep: 15 minutes | Cook: none

Per serving : 259 CAL | 1.3G FAT | 0.2G SAT FAT | 63G CARBS | 42.2G SUGAR | 4.9G FIBER | 6.3G PROTEIN | 40MG SODIUM

Ingredients

1⅔ cups large broccoli florets
2 apples, halved
1 zucchini, halved
1 teaspoon wheatgrass powder
small handful of crushed ice

1. Feed the broccoli, then the apples and zucchini, through a juicer.

2. Add the wheatgrass powder to the juice and whisk until smooth.

3. Fill a glass halfway with crushed ice, pour in the juice, and serve immediately.

Body Balance

Serves: 1 | Prep: 15 minutes | Cook: none

Per serving : 576 CAL | 8.3G FAT | 0.8G SAT FAT | 123.3G CARBS | 73.9G SUGAR | 13.8G FIBER | 11.9G PROTEIN | TRACE SODIUM

Ingredients

1 tablespoon flaxseed
⅓ cup pitted prunes
1 small banana, peeled and coarsely chopped
1 tablespoon wheat germ
juice of 2 large oranges
⅓ cup vanilla soy yogurt
1 cup chilled water

1. Put the flaxseed into a blender and blend until finely ground. Add the prunes, banana, and wheat germ and blend until smooth.

2. Add the orange juice and half the yogurt and blend until smooth. Add the water and blend once again.

3. Pour into a glass, add the remaining yogurt, and swirl together with a teaspoon, then serve.

Good-for-You Ginger

Ginger has been used as a natural remedy for centuries, especially for ailments involving the digestive system. Pregnant women are often encouraged to drink ginger tea to prevent morning sickness. Recent studies have shown that ginger may also help with menstrual cramps, migraines, colds, flu, and heartburn.

Ginger Energizer

Serves: 1 | Prep: 15 minutes | Cook: none

Per serving : 134 CAL | 1.2G FAT | TRACE SAT FAT | 29.7G CARBS | 16.2G SUGAR | 6.3G FIBER | 5.4G PROTEIN | 80MG SODIUM

The ginger in this oh-so-good-for-you vegetable drink will pep you up when you're feeling a little tired and your system is sluggish.

Ingredients

2 carrots, halved

4 tomatoes, coarsely chopped

1 tablespoon lemon juice

⅔ cup fresh flat-leaf parsley

1¼-inch piece fresh ginger, peeled and finely grated

small handful of crushed ice

½ cup chilled water

1. Feed the carrots through a juicer. Pour the juice into a blender, add the tomatoes and lemon juice, and blend.

2. Add the parsley (reserving a sprig to decorate), ginger, and crushed ice and blend again until smooth. Add the water and blend again.

3. Pour into a glass, garnish with the parsley sprig, and serve immediately.

Up the Anti

Serves: 1 | Prep: 15–20 minutes, plus chilling | Cook: none

Per serving : 250 CAL | 15G FAT | 3.5G SAT FAT | 18G CARBS | 18G SUGAR | 6G FIBER | 3G PROTEIN | TRACE SODIUM

Protect your body from the inside out with this fresh, fruity drink that is bursting with antioxidants, the body's natural defense team.

Ingredients

½ avocado, pitted, flesh
scooped from the skin

¾ cup blueberries

¾ cup hulled strawberries

juice of 1 tangerine or small orange

⅔ cup chilled water

small handful of crushed ice (optional)

1. Put the avocado, blueberries, strawberries, tangerine juice, and water into a blender and blend to combine.

2. Add the crushed ice, if using, and blend again until smooth.

3. Pour into a glass and serve immediately.

Avocado Benefits

Avocados may inhibit the growth of prostate cancer and, being high in oleic acid, they may also help to prevent breast cancer. They contain more of the carotenoid lutein than any other commonly consumed fruit. Lutein protects against macular degeneration and cataracts, two disabling age-related eye diseases. Eating avocados may also lower your cholesterol levels and, as an excellent source of glutathione, they even contain antiaging properties.

Pear & Raspberry Delight

Serves: 2 | Prep: 15 minutes | Cook: none

Per serving : 331 CAL | 1.5G FAT | 0.1G SAT FAT | 86G CARBS | 50.7G SUGAR | 15.9G FIBER | 3.3G PROTEIN | TRACE SODIUM

Frozen fruit and vegetables are useful to have on hand as a standby and are just as nutritionally sound as the fresh versions—or even better, because they are usually frozen soon after harvesting, locking in the maximum goodness.

Ingredients

2 large ripe Bosc pears, halved

1 cup frozen raspberries

1 cup ice-cold water

honey (optional)

4 raspberries, to decorate

1. Put the pears into a blender with the raspberries and water and blend until smooth.

2. Taste and sweeten with honey, if using, if the raspberries are a little too sharp for your taste.

3. Pour into glasses, decorate with whole raspberries threaded onto toothpicks, and serve immediately.

Winter Pick-Me-Up

Serves: 1 | Prep: 10–15 minutes | Cook: none

Per serving : 491 CAL | 3.5G FAT | 0.6G SAT FAT | 115.7G CARBS | 61.4G SUGAR | 7.8G FIBER | 8.7G PROTEIN | 80MG SODIUM

Banish the winter blues with this nutrient-packed juice that contains essential vitamins and minerals and will boost your energy levels.

Ingredients

1 parsnip, halved
2 carrots, halved
1 garlic clove
2 apples, halved
2 tablespoons rolled oats
1 tablespoon wheat germ
2 teaspoons honey
small handful of crushed ice (optional)
2 carrot sticks, to garnish

1. Feed the parsnip, carrots, and garlic through a juicer, then feed the apples through.

2. Put the oats and wheat germ into a blender and blend until finely ground. Add the honey and parsnip mixture and blend again until smooth.

3. Fill a glass halfway with crushed ice, if using. Pour in the juice, garnish with the carrot sticks, and serve immediately.

Pomegranate

As one of the most popular fruits championed for its taste, the pomegranate is also packed with nutrients, offering many positive health benefits that nourish the body. It is proven to lower cholesterol and contains a high level of vitamin C, helping the body develop a strong resistance to infectious bacteria and illnesses. Along with this, its natural sweetness boosts energy and it is also said to relieve stress.

Passionate Juice Fizz

Serves: 1 | Prep: 20 minutes | Cook: none

Per serving : 327 CAL | 3.9G FAT | 0.3G SAT FAT | 75.1G CARBS | 51.1G SUGAR | 20G FIBER | 6.7G PROTEIN | TRACE SODIUM

This exotic-tasting juice makes good use of passion fruit and pomegranate, whose seeds are embedded in the pulp and are meant to be eaten. Both fruits have delicious flavors that add pep to this sparkling juice.

Ingredients

1 pomegranate, seeds only

½ small orange, rind and pith removed, seeded, and coarsely chopped

4 passion fruits, seeds scooped out

⅔ cup sparkling mineral water

1. Put the pomegranate seeds into a blender, add the orange and three-quarters of the passion fruit seeds, then blend until smooth.

2. Pour into a glass and stir in the remaining passion fruit seeds.

3. Top up with the mineral water and serve.

Power-Boosting Beet

Serves: 1 | Prep: 10–15 minutes | Cook: none

Per serving: 570 CAL | 21.1G FAT | 0.9G SAT FAT | 96.1G CARBS | 63.5G SUGAR | 8.3G FIBER | 11.2G PROTEIN | 400MG SODIUM

With sweet beets, carrot, and apple, you won't need to add any extra sugar to this energizing drink. The walnuts add depth and texture to this vibrant juice.

Ingredients

2 beets, halved
2 large carrots, halved
2 celery stalks, halved
2-inch piece cucumber
2 red-skinned apples, halved
¼ cup walnut pieces, finely ground
small handful of crushed ice (optional)

1. Cut two wafer-thin slices off one of the beet halves and reserve.

2. Feed the beets and carrots, then the celery and cucumber, followed by the apples, through a juicer. Stir in the walnuts. Fill a glass halfway with crushed ice, if using, then pour in the juice.

3. Thread the beets slices through a toothpick, lay it on top of the glass, and serve immediately.

Plums for Vitamin C

Plums are a great source of vitamin C, which helps you to fight infection and increase iron absorption. But don't eat too many at once, because they are also known to have a laxative effect.

Apple & Plum Power Boost

Serves: 2 | Prep: 15 minutes | Cook: 15 minutes, plus chilling

Per serving : 148 CAL | 0.4G FAT | TRACE SAT FAT | 38.2G CARBS | 29.3G SUGAR | 5.8G FIBER | 1G PROTEIN | TRACE SODIUM

Cooking the fruit brings out the sweetness and adds a depth of flavor to this smoothie, which makes it seem substantial. For a quick-and-delicious vitamin boost, you could have it instead of your usual packed lunch.

Ingredients

1 ripe pear, peeled and quartered

1 apple, peeled and quartered

2 large red or dark plums, halved and pitted

4 ripe damsons (or extra plums), halved and pitted

1 cup water

slices of apple or pear, to decorate

1. Put the pear, apple, plums, damsons, and water into a small saucepan. Cover tightly, set over medium heat, and bring slowly to a boil. Remove from the heat and let cool. Chill.

2. Put the fruit and water into a food processor or blender and process until smooth.

3. Pour into glasses, decorate with slices of apple or pear, and serve.

Lychee & Pineapple Pep-Up

Serves: 1 | Prep: 20 minutes, plus cooling | Cook: none

Per serving: 280 CAL | 0.6G FAT | 0.2G SAT FAT | 70.7G CARBS | 57.9G SUGAR | 7G FIBER | 3.7G PROTEIN | 40MG SODIUM

Create a drink with the exotic flavors of Southeast Asia, using fragrant lemongrass and lychees blended with pineapple and melon.

Ingredients

1½ lemongrass stalks

¼ cup boiling water

6 lychees, peeled and pitted

½ small pineapple, peeled and cut into thick slices

¼ honeydew melon, thickly sliced and peeled

small handful of crushed ice (optional)

1. Cut the whole lemongrass stalk in half lengthwise, then widthwise. Bruise it with a rolling pin to release its flavor, then put it into a shallow bowl and add the boiling water. Cover and let cool completely, then drain, reserving the soaking water.

2. Feed the softened lemongrass, lychees, and pineapple, followed by the melon, through a juicer. Mix in the reserved soaking water.

3. Fill a glass halfway with crushed ice, if using, then pour in the juice and serve immediately with the remaining lemongrass as a stirrer.

Of course, we all want to look and feel the very best and get that must-have "glow," but how can we do this in an easy way? It's simple—choose juices and smoothies that are packed with loads of vitamin C, calcium, and antioxidants. We've got tons of great choices in this chapter, such as Kale Coco Bomb, Berry Booster, and Green Colada, to help you shine.

GLOW

Skin-Soother Smoothie

Serves: 1 | Prep: 10 minutes | Cook: none

Per serving: 466 CAL | 13.4G FAT | 2.1G SAT FAT | 87.5G CARBS | 51.1G SUGAR | 15.7G FIBER | 10.1G PROTEIN | TRACE SODIUM

Packed with healing vitamin C from the fruit, skin-protecting vitamin E from the peanut butter, and essential fatty acids (EFAs) from the flaxseed, this spectacular layered drink might just be your skin's new best friend.

Ingredients

Banana layer

1 banana, peeled and coarsely chopped
1 tablespoon smooth peanut butter
1 tablespoon soy yogurt

Blueberry layer

1 cup blueberries
juice of ½ lemon

Kiwi layer

3 kiwis, peeled and coarsely chopped
1 tablespoon ground flaxseed

1. Put all the ingredients for the banana layer into a blender and blend until smooth. Transfer to a large lipped measuring cup and rinse the blender goblet.

2. To make the blueberry layer, put the blueberries and lemon juice into the blender and blend until smooth. Transfer to a separate large lipped measuring cup and rinse the blender goblet.

3. To make the kiwi layer, put the kiwis into the blender with the flaxseed and blend until smooth. Layer the three smoothie mixtures into a large glass and serve immediately.

Why Not Try?

Coconut yogurt also works well here,
but substitute the yogurt with a
splash of cold water, if necessary.

Thai Sunrise

Hail the Kale

Thai Sunrise

Serves: 1 | Prep: 10–15 minutes | Cook: none

Per serving : 148 CAL | 0.6G FAT | TRACE SAT FAT | 38G CARBS | 23.8G SUGAR | 7.4G FIBER | 2.6G PROTEIN | 40MG SODIUM

Ingredients

1¾ cups spinach
6 fresh Thai basil leaves
1 cup chilled water
1 pear, halved
4 fresh lychees, peeled and pitted
1 thin slice fresh ginger, peeled
juice of ½ lime
1 Thai basil sprig, to garnish

1. Put the spinach, basil, and water into a blender and blend until smooth.

2. Add the pear, lychees, ginger, and lime juice, then blend until smooth. Serve immediately, garnished with a Thai basil sprig.

Hail the Kale

Serves: 1 | Prep: 10–15 minutes| Cook: none

Per serving : 100 CAL | 10.0G FAT | 1.0G SAT FAT | 10.0G CARBS | 5.0G SUGAR | 1.0G FIBER | 1.0G PROTEIN | TRACE SODIUM

Ingredients

½ cup shredded green curly kale
2 x 2-inch piece of coconut meat
1½ cups chilled almond milk
1 tablespoon sunflower seeds
¼ teaspoon ground cinnamon
¼ teaspoon ground cinnamon, to garnish

1. Put the kale into a blender.

2. Add the coconut, almond milk, sunflower seeds, and cinnamon, then blend until smooth and creamy (this might take a little longer than usual due to the coconut).

3. Serve immediately, sprinkled with cinnamon.

Kiwi Quencher

Serves: 1 | Prep: 15 minutes | Cook: none

Per serving: 414 CAL | 2.5G FAT | 0.2G SAT FAT | 103.5G CARBS | 67.5G SUGAR | 20.6G FIBER | 7.3G PROTEIN | TRACE SODIUM

What a combo: cool, jewel-like kiwis blended with naturally juicy green grapes and thirst-quenching crisp, fresh lettuce.

Ingredients

½ head of romaine lettuce

4 kiwis, peeled

¾ cup green grapes

1 large pear, halved

small handful of crushed ice, to serve (optional)

1. Peel off a lettuce leaf and reserve.

2. Feed the kiwis and grapes, then the lettuce and pear, through a juicer.

3. Fill a glass halfway with crushed ice, if using, then pour in the juice. Decorate with the reserved lettuce leaf and serve immediately.

Ruby Fruit Reviver

Serves: 1 | Prep: 15–20 minutes | Cook: none

Per serving : 162 CAL | 0.8G FAT | TRACE SAT FAT | 40.4G CARBS | 25.5G SUGAR | 7.3G FIBER | 3.4G PROTEIN | TRACE SODIUM

There's nothing more refreshing than locally grown strawberries in season, so this smoothie is best enjoyed in the early summer. Shop carefully for strawberries that really smell and taste as they should—biggest doesn't necessarily mean best.

Ingredients

1 ruby red grapefruit, rind and a little pith removed, seeded, and coarsely chopped

¼ cucumber, coarsely chopped

1 cup hulled strawberries

small handful of crushed ice (optional)

1. Put the grapefruit and cucumber into a blender and blend until smooth.

2. Add the strawberries and crushed ice, if using, and blend again until smooth and combined.

3. Pour into a glass and serve immediately.

Freezing Bananas

To freeze bananas, peel them, then freeze them on a tray for 30 minutes, spaced well apart. When frozen, transfer to plastic food bags or containers. Use within 3–4 months.

Kale Coco Bomb

Serves: 1 | Prep: 10–15 minutes | Cook: none

Per serving : 133 CAL | 2.4G FAT | 0.4G SAT FAT | 28.1G CARBS | 13.1G SUGAR | 5.1G FIBER | 4.3G PROTEIN | TRACE SODIUM

This creamy smoothie tastes like a decadent treat, but with nutrient-rich kale and raw cacao powder, it is actually good for you. It's also a good way to use extra bananas, stored frozen in the freezer.

Ingredients

¾ cup shredded green curly kale

1 cup chilled water

1 teaspoon hemp seeds or hempseed oil

1 frozen banana

1 teaspoon raw cacao powder

¼ vanilla bean, seeds scraped

small pinch of raw cacao powder, to garnish

1. Put the kale into a blender with the water and blend until smooth.

2. Add the hemp seeds, banana, cacao powder, and vanilla seeds and blend again until smooth and creamy.

3. Pour into a glass and serve immediately, garnished with a pinch of raw cacao.

Powerful Mango

Serves: 1 | Prep: 15–20 minutes | Cook: none

Per serving: 460 CAL | 2G FAT | 0.3G SAT FAT | 118.9G CARBS | 98.2G SUGAR | 4G FIBER | 4.6G PROTEIN | TRACE SODIUM

The mango adds a delicious tropical flavor to this refreshing juice. If you can't get clementines, use mandarin oranges instead, but be sure to seed them. You may need to add an extra teaspoon of honey, because clementines are sweeter.

Ingredients

2 clementines, rind and a little pith removed

1 mango, pitted and peeled

2 apples, halved

small handful of crushed ice, to serve (optional)

chilled water, to taste

1 teaspoon honey

1. Feed the clementines, mango, and apples through a juicer.

2. Fill a glass halfway with crushed ice, if using. Pour in the juice, top up with water to taste, stir in the honey, and serve immediately.

Minted Melon Drink

Serves: 1 | Prep: 15 minutes | Cook: none

Per serving: 153 CAL | 0.6G FAT | 0.2G SAT FAT | 38.8G CARBS | 32.7G SUGAR | 0.9G FIBER | 2.6G PROTEIN | 80MG SODIUM

Did you ever think that it was a waste to throw away the broccoli stem and half the weight of the vegetable? The stem has just as many nutrients as the florets, yet it is often trashed, although it is a valuable addition to soups and juices.

Ingredients

½ honeydew melon, thickly
sliced and peeled

5 fresh mint sprigs

½ lime, rind and a little pith removed

1-inch slice of broccoli stem

small handful of crushed ice (optional)

1. Feed the melon and mint, then the lime and broccoli, through a juicer.

2. Fill a glass halfway with crushed ice, if using, then pour in the juice and serve immediately.

Give Green Juice a Chance

Green juicing is no longer the preserve of movie stars, supermodels, and vegans. Everyone's gone mad for it, and no wonder. If you want to look after your health, well-being, weight, and appearance, there is surely no easier way to do it than by incorporating juicing into your diet. Always buy the best-quality, freshest products you can find—they contain more nutrients and flavor. Avoid anything discolored or wilted, which will have lost the B vitamins, vitamin C, and enzymes.

Berry Booster

Serves: 1 | Prep: 15 minutes| Cook: none

Per serving : 129 CAL | 1.3G FAT | TRACE SAT FAT | 29.8G CARBS | 15.2G SUGAR | 13G FIBER | 3.2G PROTEIN | TRACE SODIUM

Think of this juice as the ultimate beauty treatment. It will rehydrate your skin and plump up and reduce wrinkles, and the vitamin C-loaded berries will help clear up any annoying acne and blemishes.

Ingredients

1 cup hulled strawberries
(one reserved unhulled)

¾ cup raspberries

⅔ cup blackberries

¾ cup chilled water

small handful of crushed ice (optional)

1. Cut the reserved unhulled strawberry in half and reserve one half, along with a raspberry and a blackberry.

2. Put the remaining strawberries, raspberries, blackberries, and water into a blender and blend until smooth. Fill a glass halfway with crushed ice, if using, then pour in the berry juice.

3. Thread the reserved fruit onto a wooden skewer to make a stirrer, then serve with the juice.

Berry Bonus

Most of us know that berries contain vitamin C, but did you know that raspberries also contain manganese—which helps with the metabolism of carbohydrates—proteins, and cholesterol and helps to keep our bones healthy?

Broccoli

One cup of broccoli contains 135 percent of the daily amount of vitamin C the body needs, protecting the skin from blemishes and wrinkles and providing a soothed complexion and healthy glow. Broccoli also contains a large amount of the nutrient carotene, which offers antioxidant protection, helping to maintain the skin's glow, while protecting and cleansing the body in general.

Boost It

To make this delicious juice even more nutritious, add 1 teaspoon of spirulina for a calcium hit.

Beet It

Serves: 1 | Prep: 10–15 minutes | Cook: none

Per serving : 191 CAL | 1.2G FAT | 0.1G SAT FAT | 44.6G CARBS | 27.6G SUGAR | 2.6G FIBER | 6.1G PROTEIN | 200MG SODIUM

Earthy and sweet beets bring a lot to the table. The leaves are also nutritious and should not be discarded—beet greens can be enjoyed in the same way as spinach.

Ingredients

2 cups arugula
1 small head of radicchio
1 cup beet greens
1 green apple, halved
1 beet, halved

1. Feed the arugula, radicchio, beet leaves, apple, and beet through a juicer.

2. Stir well, pour into a glass, and serve immediately.

Green Apple & Kiwi Juice

Serves: 2 | Prep: 10–15 minutes | Cook: none

Per serving : 160 CAL | 0.8G FAT | 0.1G SAT FAT | 41.5G CARBS | 27.3G SUGAR | 21.5G FIBER | 2.2G PROTEIN | TRACE SODIUM

Apples are rich in vitamin C, which is great for maintaining the elasticity of your skin and keeping your hair healthy and shiny. The addition of cucumber will benefit your skin, helping to keep it clear and free of blemishes.

Ingredients

2 green cooking apples,
such as Granny Smith, halved

½ cucumber, coarsely chopped

2 kiwis, peeled and coarsely chopped

½ lemon, rind and pith removed, seeded,
and coarsely chopped

¾-inch piece fresh ginger, peeled and
coarsely chopped

1. Feed all of the ingredients through a juicer.

2. Transfer the juice to tall glasses and serve immediately.

Blackberry Blaster

Serves: 1 | Prep: 15 minutes | Cook: none

Per serving : 333 CAL | 3.6G FAT | 0.3G SAT FAT | 74.6G CARBS | 43.5G SUGAR | 6.5G FIBER | 9.9G PROTEIN | TRACE SODIUM

Banish those morning blues with this cinnamon-spiced dairy-free juice. It's bursting with vitamins and minerals, and will keep you energized until lunchtime.

Ingredients

3 large red-skinned plums,
halved and pitted

¾ cup red curly kale

1 pear, halved

¾ cup blackberries

3 tablespoons wheat germ

¼ teaspoon ground cinnamon (optional)

small handful of crushed ice

¼–⅓ cup chilled water

1. Feed the plums, then the kale, followed by the pear, through a juicer. Pour the juice into a blender. Add the blackberries (reserving one to decorate), wheat germ, cinnamon, if using, and crushed ice and blend until smooth.

2. Add the water to taste and blend again until smooth. Pour into a glass.

3. Thread a blackberry onto a toothpick, add it to the glass, and serve immediately.

Blackberries: Nature's Aspirin

Energy-boosting blackberries are a good source of vitamin C, folates, and fiber. More unusually, they also contain salicylates, a natural aspirin-like compound, so if you are allergic to aspirin, keep away from this fruit.

Boost It

Boost this juice's nutritional power and get your skin glowing by adding 2 teaspoons of acai powder.

Sprout Tonic

Serves: 1 | Prep: 10–15 minutes | Cook: none

Per serving: 162 CAL | 2.7G FAT | 0G SAT FAT | 31.8G CARBS | 15.2G SUGAR | 5G FIBER | 4.2G PROTEIN | 200MG SODIUM

Brussels sprouts appear occasionally on a Christmas dinner plate, but drinking them in a smoothie like this means you can eat your greens all year round.

Ingredients
4 Brussels sprouts
¾ cup beet greens
½ cup Swiss chard
1 cup unsweetened rice milk

1. Put the Brussels sprouts, beet greens, and Swiss chard into a blender.

2. Pour in the rice milk and blend until smooth and creamy.

3. Pour into a glass and serve immediately.

Kiwi

Kiwis are full of omega-3, which is important in preventing an array of skin diseases and protecting the health of cell membranes. As a strong provider of vitamin C and vitamin E, kiwis help to maintain the skin's moisture and aids the healing of cuts and scars.

Mango & Lime Bone Builder

Serves: 1 | Prep: 15 minutes | Cook: none

Per serving: 346 CAL | 10G FAT | 1.7G SAT FAT | 57.6G CARBS | 46.4G SUGAR | 8.5G FIBER | 11G PROTEIN | 40MG SODIUM

The natural sweetness of mango perfectly balances the kale in this pretty, green-speckled drink, which will boost your calcium intake, keeping your bones strong.

Ingredients

1 tablespoon sesame seeds

juice of ⅓ lime

⅓ cup shredded green curly kale

1 mango, peeled, pitted, and coarsely chopped

1 cup unsweetened rice, almond, or soy milk

small handful of crushed ice

1. Put the sesame seeds into a blender and blend until finely ground.

2. Add the lime juice, kale, and mango and blend until well combined.

3. Add the milk and crushed ice and blend again until smooth. Pour into a glass and serve immediately.

Good for Bones

The calcium-boosting sesame seeds and kale help to maintain bone strength and muscle function.

Did You Know?

Coconut milk comes in two forms. The thinner milk, available in a carton, has a lower fat content than the thicker milk that comes in a can. Scoop off the fat in a can and use in recipes calling for coconut cream. The thin milk is ideal for juices and smoothies or as a replacement for dairy milk.

Green Colada

Serves: 1 | Prep: 10–15 minutes | Cook: none

Per serving: 115 CAL | 5.4G FAT | 4G SAT FAT | 14.5G CARBS | 5.3G SUGAR | 1.7G FIBER | 4.9G PROTEIN | 160MG SODIUM

This elegant and deliciously refreshing drink is an excellent calcium booster and provides the vitamins and minerals needed for a healthy and glowing complexion.

Ingredients

3½ cups spinach, coarsely chopped
⅓ cucumber, coarsely chopped
⅙ cup fresh mint
1 cup coconut milk
⅛ teaspoon flaxseed
1 teaspoon chlorophyll powder
1 fresh mint sprig,
to garnish
crushed ice, to serve

1. Feed the spinach and cucumber through a juicer with the mint.

2. Stir through the coconut milk, flaxseed, and chlorophyll powder until thoroughly combined.

3. Fill a glass with crushed ice, pour in the juice, garnish with a mint sprig, and serve immediately.

Fresh & Fruity

Serves: 1 | Prep: 10–15 minutes | Cook: none

Per serving: 219 CAL | 1.1G FAT | TRACE SAT FAT | 55.3G CARBS | 38.9G SUGAR | 10.2G FIBER | 3.1G PROTEIN | TRACE SODIUM

The pineapple in this smoothie will help prevent constipation and promote a clear complexion, and the blackberries and blueberries are high in the antioxidants that combat the free radicals known to damage the skin's youthful elasticity.

Ingredients

½ small pineapple, peeled and coarsely chopped

⅔ cup blackberries

⅔ cup blueberries

1 teaspoon goji berries, coarsely chopped, to decorate

1. Put the pineapple into a blender with the blackberries and blueberries and blend until smooth.

2. Pour into a glass, sprinkle with the chopped goji berries, and serve.

Cranberry Soother

Serves: 1 | Prep: 10 minutes | Cook: none

Per serving : 205 CAL | 3.2G FAT | 1.9G SAT FAT | 42.7G CARBS | 29.4G SUGAR | 5.6G FIBER | 4.4G PROTEIN | 40MG SODIUM

Help to protect your body with this wonderfully colorful and tasty drink. It's a great way to encourage your children to eat more vitamin C-packed fruit, too.

Ingredients

1½ cups cranberries

juice of 1 orange

⅓ cup plain yogurt

2 teaspoons honey

1. Put the cranberries and orange juice into a blender and blend until smooth.

2. Add the yogurt and honey and blend again.

3. Pour into a glass and serve immediately.

Grape Nutrient Booster

Serves: 1 | Prep: 15 minutes | Cook: none

Per serving : 416 CAL | 5.7G FAT | 0.9G SAT FAT | 94.5G CARBS | 62.6G SUGAR | 6.3G FIBER | 9.3G PROTEIN | 40MG SODIUM

Naturally sweet pears and grapes are a terrific way to disguise the taste of
nutritious vegetables, such as cabbage, in a juice. And because the pumpkin seeds
in this drink are finely ground, no one will know they are there.

Ingredients

2 pears, halved

¼ small head of savoy cabbage,
coarsely chopped

1 tablespoon pumpkin seeds

1 cup seedless green grapes

small handful of crushed ice (optional)

1. Feed the pears and cabbage through a juicer.

2. Put the pumpkin seeds into a blender and blend until finely ground,
then add the grapes and crushed ice, if using, and blend. Pour in the pear
juice mix and blend until smooth.

3. Pour into a glass and serve immediately.

Cabbage Nutrition

Savoy cabbage is a storehouse of phytochemicals and powerful antioxidants, which are thought to help protect against cancer. It also contains a huge range of vitamins and minerals, not to mention beta-carotene and the amino acid glutamine (an anti-inflammatory).

Making a delicious smoothie when you have digestive problems can have huge benefits. Not only can it help relax, comfort, and soothe you as you drink, but it can have a range of real health benefits for your digestive tract. This chapter is full of ideal choices, such as Mellow Mr. Green, Cucumber Soother, and Broccoli Booster, that are kind on your stomach but full of flavor.

SOOTHE

Melon & Coconut Mojito

Serves: 1 | Prep: 10–15 minutes | Cook: none

Per serving: 265 CAL | 17.3G FAT | 14.9G SAT FAT | 28.8G CARBS | 21G SUGAR | 7.4G FIBER | 4G PROTEIN | TRACE SODIUM

This fresh and fruity smoothie will bring back happy memories of hot summer days. With cooling mint and melon and refreshing tropical coconut and mango, it will be hard to beat as a hot weather soother.

Ingredients

¾ cup spinach

2 x 2-inch piece of coconut meat

1 cup chilled water

¼ small cantaloupe, peeled and seeded

1 tablespoon chopped fresh mint

juice of ½ lime

⅓ cup pitted, peeled, and coarsely chopped mango

1 mango slice, pitted and peeled, to garnish

crushed ice, to serve

1. Put the spinach, coconut, and water into a blender and blend until smooth.

2. Add the melon, mint, lime juice, and mango and blend again until smooth and creamy.

3. Pour over crushed ice, if using, and serve immediately, garnished with the mango slice.

Greek Green

Mellow Mr. Green

Greek Green

Serves: 1 | Prep: 10–15 minutes | Cook: none

Per serving: 308 CAL | 24G FAT | 13.2G SAT FAT | 12.8G CARBS | 6.7G SUGAR | 4.8G FIBER | 13.9G PROTEIN | 40MG SODIUM

Ingredients

¼ cup shredded curly green kale

1 cup chilled water

¼ vanilla bean, seeds scraped

½ cup Greek-style yogurt

2 x 1½-inch piece of fresh coconut meat

1 tablespoon almond butter

1. Put the kale into a blender with the water and blend until smooth and creamy.

2. Add the vanilla seeds to the blender with the yogurt, coconut, and almond butter, then blend until smooth. Serve immediately.

Mellow Mr. Green

Serves: 1 | Prep: 15 minutes | Cook: none

Per serving: 306 CAL | 21.8G FAT | 15G SAT FAT | 28.1G CARBS | 19.3G SUGAR | 5.2G FIBER | 6.3G PROTEIN | 40MG SODIUM

Ingredients

½ cup arugula

1 cup chilled water

1 kiwi, peeled and coarsely chopped

1 cup peeled, seeded, and coarsely chopped canteloupe

3 tablespoons unsweetened coconut cream

2 teaspoons smooth peanut butter

1. Put the arugula and water into a blender and blend until smooth.

2. Add the kiwi and melon to the blender with the coconut cream and peanut butter and blend until creamy. Serve immediately.

Bee Pollen & Nectarine Soother

Serves: 2 | Prep: 15 minutes | Cook: none

Per serving: 163 CAL | 3.2G FAT | 1.8G SAT FAT | 28.7G CARBS | 22.8G SUGAR | 2.6G FIBER | 7.3G PROTEIN | 40MG SODIUM

Nutritious bee pollen adds an intriguing touch to this nifty and nourishing nectarine milk shake. Milk and plain yogurt team up to create a calcium-rich base, and the honey adds a touch of natural sweetness.

Ingredients

2 ripe nectarines, pitted and quartered

1 cup low-fat milk

2 tablespoons Greek-style plain yogurt

1 tablespoon bee pollen

1 teaspoon honey

handful of ice cubes

1 teaspoon bee pollen, to decorate

2 slices nectarine, to decorate

1. Put the nectarines, milk, yogurt, bee pollen, and honey into a blender and blend until smooth. Add the ice cubes and blend again until completely blended.

2. Pour the milk shake into chilled glasses and decorate each with the bee pollen and a slice of nectarine. Serve immediately.

Why Not Try?

If you like your smoothies a little
sweeter, add some more honey
to the recipe.

Supersmoothie

Serves: 1 | Prep: 10–15 minutes | Cook: none

Per serving : 308 CAL | 17.2G FAT | 2.4G SAT FAT | 40.3G CARBS | 15.2G SUGAR | 12.7G FIBER | 5.3G PROTEIN | 40MG SODIUM

The avocado is a nutrient-dense food that helps the body to absorb fat-soluble nutrients. If that isn't enough to persuade you to add avocados to smoothies, do it because it makes them creamy and soothing.

Ingredients

1 cup spinach

1 cup cooled licorice tea

½ avocado, pitted, flesh scooped from the skin

1 frozen banana

1 teaspoon chia seeds

½ teaspoon chia seeds, to garnish

1. Put the spinach and licorice tea into a blender and blend until smooth.

2. Chop the avocado, add it to the blender with the banana and chia seeds, and blend until smooth and creamy.

3. Serve immediately, garnished with a sprinkling of chia seeds.

Freezing Fruit

When you have an abundance of fruit and vegetables, freeze them in small servings, and they'll be ready when you need them for your smoothies.

Powerful
Pumpkin Seeds

These little seeds are really
nutritious, and even in small servings,
they provide a significant amount of
minerals, especially zinc and iron.

Berry Power

Serves: 1 | Prep: 15 minutes | Cook: none

Per serving: 641 CAL | 33.8G FAT | 3.7G SAT FAT | 72.7G CARBS | 41.8G SUGAR | 19.9G FIBER | 22.1G PROTEIN | 40MG SODIUM

Breakfast is arguably the most important meal of the day, and this shake includes plenty of vital nutrients. It's quick to make, tasty, and filling, but it won't leave you feeling heavy.

Ingredients

2 tablespoons pumpkin seeds
2 tablespoons flaxseed
3 tablespoons slivered almonds
1 cup raspberries
¾ cup blueberries
1 cup vanilla soy yogurt
½ cup chilled water

1. Put the pumpkin seeds, flaxseed, and almonds into a blender and blend until finely ground.

2. Add the raspberries, blueberries, yogurt, and chilled water and blend until smooth.

3. Pour into a glass and serve.

Plum Power

Serves: 1 | Prep: 10–15 minutes | Cook: 20 minutes, plus cooling

Per serving : 289 CAL | 3.6G FAT | 2.5G SAT FAT | 53.9G CARBS | 53.7G SUGAR | 2.1G FIBER | 9.9G PROTEIN | 120MG SODIUM

This pretty, icy fruit shake will cool you down while giving you a quick burst of energy from the plums and honey and more sustainable energy from the yogurt.

Ingredients

2 plums, pitted

⅓ cup water

2 teaspoons honey

2 scoops plain frozen yogurt

1 Italian almond or pistachio biscotti, crumbled, to decorate (optional)

¼ plum, pitted, to decorate (optional)

1. Put the plums, water, and honey into a small saucepan over medium heat. Stir, cover tightly, reduce the heat to low, and simmer for 15 minutes, until the plums have split and are soft. Let cool.

2. Pour the mixture into a blender, then add the frozen yogurt and blend until smooth.

3. Pour into a glass, sprinkle with the biscotti, if using, decorate the rim with the plum, if using, and serve immediately.

Grape & Lychee Reviver

Serves: 1 | Prep: 15 minutes | Cook: none

Per serving : 413 CAL | 15.6G FAT | 2.3G SAT FAT | 72.8G CARBS | 54.6G SUGAR | 8.3G FIBER | 6.2G PROTEIN | 40MG SODIUM

Go Asian with fragrant lychees, thought by the Chinese to be the symbol of love. Blend them with creamy, smooth avocado and naturally sweet grapes for the perfect pick-me-up to rehydrate and fight fatigue.

Ingredients

2 cups green grapes

2 cups young spinach

½ ripe avocado, pitted, flesh scooped from the skin

5 lychees, peeled and pitted

small handful of crushed ice

½ cup chilled water

1 slice of avocado to serve (optional)

1. Feed the grapes and spinach through a juicer.

2. Pour the juice into a blender, add the avocado, lychees, and crushed ice, and blend until smooth.

3. Add the water and blend again. Pour into a glass, add the avocado slice, if using, and serve immediately.

Grape Nutrition

Grapes are a good source of potassium; however, based on weight, they provide only one-twentieth of the vitamin C of kiwi.

Manuka Honey

Manuka honey is known for its immune
boosting abilities and nutritional benefits.
It slowly releases the glycogen that the
body needs to function during sleep,
promoting a deeper and more restful sleep.
Heart disease, diabetes, and arthritis are
accentuated by a lack of proper rest, so
incorporating manuka honey within your
diet can decrease these risks.

Vanilla, Almond & Banana Smoothie

Serves: 2 | Prep: 5 minutes | Cook: none

Per serving: 330 CAL | 18.1G FAT | 1.4G SAT FAT | 31.4G CARBS | 24.4G SUGAR | 6.4G FIBER | 9.4G PROTEIN | 80MG SODIUM

This protein-packed smoothie is sweetened only with dates, but it tastes as sweet and delicious as the best milk shake you've ever had.

Ingredients

1 cup almond milk

¼ cup almond butter

1 banana, peeled and coarsely chopped

4 pitted dates

1 teaspoon vanilla extract

8–10 ice cubes

1. Put all the ingredients into a blender and blend until smooth.

2. Pour into two glasses and serve immediately.

Why Not Try?

Melon can be used instead of the pear or apple and will keep this juice cool and soothing.

Cucumber Soother

Serves: 1 | Prep: 10–15 minutes | Cook: none

Per serving: 259 CAL | 0.8G FAT | TRACE SAT FAT | 67.9G CARBS | 43.1G SUGAR | 3.2G FIBER | 2.2G PROTEIN | TRACE SODIUM

This light, fresh-tasting juice made with the addition of soothing aloe vera gel can help to reduce digestive problems, such as heartburn.

Ingredients

1 large pear, halved

⅓ cucumber, coarsely chopped

1 green apple, halved

¼ cup fresh mint

1 tablespoon aloe vera gel

crushed ice, to serve (optional)

1 slice of cucumber,
to garnish

1 fresh mint sprig,
to garnish

1. Feed the pear, cucumber, and apple through a juicer with the mint.

2. Stir through the aloe vera gel until combined. Pour the crushed ice, if using, into a glass, then pour in the juice.

3. Serve immediately, garnished with a cucumber slice and a sprig of mint.

Stomach Soother

Serves: 1 | Prep: 15 minutes | Cook: none

Per serving: 259 CAL | 0.7G FAT | TRACE SAT FAT | 69.8G CARBS | 48.8G SUGAR | 2.2G FIBER | 3.5G PROTEIN | TRACE SODIUM

Pineapple juice is great for improving digestion and soothing an upset stomach, and its effects are reinforced here with fresh ginger. The healing enzyme bromelain reduces bruising, so it can help with recovery from an injury.

Ingredients

⅓ sweet pineapple, peeled and cut into thick slices

1 lemon, rind and most of the pith removed, halved

¾-inch piece fresh ginger, peeled

1 pineapple leaf, to decorate (optional)

1. Feed the pineapple, lemon, and ginger through a juicer.

2. Pour into a glass, add the pineapple leaf as a stirrer, if using, and serve. Remove the pineapple leaf before drinking.

Turbo Recharger

Serves: 1 | Prep: 20 minutes | Cook: none

Per serving : 413 CAL | 3.8G FAT | 0.8G SAT FAT | 94.7G CARBS | 70.9G SUGAR | 10.2G FIBER | 9.8G PROTEIN | 0.2G SODIUM

This smoothie includes everything you need to revitalize your body: rehydrating melon, energy-boosting banana, vitamin C-packed grapes, and iron-rich watercress.

Ingredients

⅛ honeydew melon, peeled, seeded, and coarsely chopped

1 banana, peeled and coarsely chopped

1 kiwi, peeled and coarsely chopped

¾ cup seedless green grapes

small handful of watercress or arugula

½ cup unsweetened rice, almond, or soy milk

small handful of crushed ice (optional)

1. Put the melon, banana, kiwi, grapes, and watercress into a blender and blend until smooth.

2. Add the milk and crushed ice, if using, and blend again until smooth.

3. Pour into a glass and serve immediately.

Wow, Watercress

Watercress is packed with antioxidants, minerals, and vitamins C and K. It's also rich in chlorophyll, which assists with the oxygenation of blood cells.

Go Nuts

Serves: 1 | Prep: 10–15 minutes | Cook: none

Per serving : 546 CAL | 32.1G FAT | 5.6G SAT FAT | 67.5G CARBS | 49.6G SUGAR | 14.9G FIBER | 7.8G PROTEIN | 120MG SODIUM

Smooth and creamy meets sweet and nutty in this delicious dairy-free pick-me-up. The addition of plump and juicy Medjool dates, grown on a tree known as "the tree of life," lifts this smoothie right out of the ordinary.

Ingredients

½ avocado, pitted,
flesh scooped from the skin

4 Brazil nuts

3 Medjool dates

¼-inch slice of fresh ginger, peeled

1½ cups almond milk

¼ teaspoon ground cinnamon

crushed ice, to serve (optional)

1. Put the avocado, nuts, dates, and ginger into a blender and blend until smooth and creamy.

2. Pour in the almond milk, add the cinnamon, and blend again until smooth.

3. Pour the smoothie over crushed ice, if using, and serve immediately.

Cinnamon Power

Cinnamon helps to regulate blood sugar, making it a great addition for diabetics and hypoglycemics.

Bananas

Bananas are natural mood enhancers, rich in tryptophan, which the body converts into serotonin. This provokes a happier mood, soothing stress and relieving symptoms of PMS and SAD. Bananas are also antacids, lowering the distress associated with heartburn, stomach aches, and acid reflux.

Sensational Strawberries

Strawberries have more vitamin C than any other red berries and so have great antiviral and antibacterial properties. They are rich in beta-carotene, which is converted by the body into vitamin A. Their natural fruit sugars also give the body an early-morning energy boost. They also contain lignin, which may help reduce blood cholesterol.

Berry Whip

Serves: 4 | Prep: 10–15 minutes | Cook: none

Per serving: 213 CAL | 12.8G FAT | 2.4G SAT FAT | 23.2G CARBS | 11.6G SUGAR | 3.5G FIBER | 4.7G PROTEIN | 80MG SODIUM

Frozen berries are a healthy and handy freezer staple. Here, they're blended with protein-boosting cashew nuts and Brazil nuts for a delicious shake.

Ingredients

¾ cup frozen sliced strawberries
¾ cup frozen blueberries
12 Brazil nuts
⅓ cup cashew nut pieces
⅓ cup rolled oats
2 cups almond milk
2 tablespoons maple syrup

1. Put the strawberries, blueberries, Brazil nuts, and cashew nut pieces into a blender. Sprinkle with the oats, then pour in half the almond milk. Blend until smooth.

2. Add the remaining milk and the maple syrup and blend until smooth.

3. Pour into four glasses and serve immediately with spoons. As the drink stands, the blueberries will almost set the liquid, but as soon as you stir it, it will turn to liquid again.

Berry Breakfast

Serves: 1 | Prep: 10 minutes | Cook: none

Per serving: 290 CAL | 5G FAT | 0.5G SAT FAT | 52.7G CARBS | 20.2G SUGAR | 14.6G FIBER | 10.1G PROTEIN | TRACE SODIUM

This soothing breakfast-in-a-glass is packed with sustaining nutrients to keep up your energy levels all morning and see you through until lunchtime.

Ingredients

1⅓ cups hulled strawberries
(one reserved and halved, to decorate)

¾ cup raspberries

⅓ cup unsweetened
rice, almond, or soy milk

⅓ cup unsweetened muesli

1. Put the strawberries and raspberries into a blender and blend to a puree. Add the milk and muesli and blend again until almost smooth.

3. Pour into a glass, top with the reserved strawberry half, and serve.

Why Not Try?

For another fruity option, try papaya
in place of the pineapple.

Pineapple Pump

Serves: 1 | Prep: 10–15 minutes | Cook: none

Per serving: 233 CAL | 2.1G FAT | 0.2G SAT FAT | 49.6G CARBS | 24.9G SUGAR | 4.8G FIBER | 10.9G PROTEIN | 240MG SODIUM

Protein- and mineral-rich wheatgrass really pumps up the nutrition in this vibrant green energizer. Celery, curly kale, and pineapple will boost your intake of vitamins, minerals, and fiber and will really get your digestive juices flowing.

Ingredients

5 celery stalks, coarsely chopped

3 cups shredded curly green kale

1 cup peeled, cored, and coarsely chopped fresh pineapple

1 bunch of mint

1 teaspoon wheatgrass powder

1 small slice of fresh pineapple, to garnish

1 kale leaf, to garnish

1. Feed the celery, kale, and pineapple through a juicer funnel with the mint.

2. Stir in the wheatgrass powder until combined.

3. Serve immediately, garnished with the slice of pineapple and a kale leaf.

Broccoli Booster

Serves: 1 | Prep: 10–15 minutes | Cook: none

Per serving : 308 CAL | 7.7G FAT | 1.7G SAT FAT | 56.8G CARBS | 31.9G SUGAR | 9.3G FIBER | 13G PROTEIN | 80MG SODIUM

Bananas suppress acid in the digestive tract, which alleviates heartburn and helps fight ulcers. They also contain a soluble fiber that aids the elimination process, so they are great for boosting digestive health.

Ingredients

2 cups coarsely chopped broccoli stems

2¾ cups spinach

1 cup chilled water

1 frozen banana

1 tablespoon pumpkin seed butter

1 tablespoon manuka honey

1. Put the broccoli into a blender with the spinach and water and blend until smooth.

2. Add the banana, pumpkin seed butter, and honey, then blend again until smooth and creamy. Serve immediately.

Seed Butter

There are several seed butters to try,
all with great benefits, so look for
sesame, hemp, and pumpkin butters.

Beat the Morning Blues

Serves: 1 | Prep: 10–15 minutes | Cook: none

Per serving : 294 CAL | 5.3G FAT | 0.4G SAT FAT | 62G CARBS | 40.4G SUGAR | 5.9G FIBER | 5.4G PROTEIN | TRACE SODIUM

Full of vitamin C-packed, antioxidant-rich delicious blueberries, this hearty nondairy juice is a truly supercharged breakfast immunity boost.

Ingredients

1 pear, halved

1 cup blueberries

½ cup soy yogurt

½ teaspoon agave syrup

2 teaspoons slivered almonds, toasted

1. Feed the pear through a juicer. Pour the juice into a blender, add the blueberries, and blend until smooth.

2. Add the yogurt and agave syrup and blend until smooth.

3. Pour into a glass, sprinkle with the almonds, and serve.

Cleanse your body and introduce juices such as Big Apple Detox, Fennel Flush, Green Tea Punch, and Spinach Aid to help you feel revitalized, toxin-free, and healthy. The recipes in this chapter are not just supertasty but will also provide essential carbohydrates, fiber, plant chemicals, and plenty of vitamin C to help you feel like you're running at optimum efficiency.

DETOX

Pineapple & Nettle Smoothie

Serves: 2 | Prep: 15–20 mins | Cook: none

Per serving : 351 CAL | 2.4G FAT | 0.2G SAT FAT | 83.1G CARBS | 53.1G SUGAR | 12.8G FIBER | 6.9G PROTEIN | TRACE SODIUM

Nettles are said to help purify the blood—they're certainly rich in iron—and consuming them with fruits that contain vitamin C, such as pineapple and lemon, helps the body to absorb this important mineral.

Ingredients
Nettle layer
5 cups nettle leaves, rinsed and blanched

1 apple, cored and coarsely chopped

1 lemon, peeled and coarsely chopped

2 pitted dates, quartered

¼ teaspoon dried ginger

½ cup orange juice

Pineapple layer
⅛ fresh pineapple, peeled and cored

⅔ cup soy yogurt

⅓ cup rolled oats

1. To make the nettle layer, put all the ingredients into a blender and blend until smooth. Transfer to a large lipped measuring cup and rinse the blender goblet.

2. To make the pineapple layer, chop the pineapple into bite-size pieces. Put into the blender, add the yogurt and oats, and blend until smooth.

3. Layer the two mixtures in two large glasses and serve immediately.

Nutritious Nettles

Once blanched and blended, nettles can't sting you, but handle carefully before you steam them. The stinging barbs are on the stems and underside of the leaves.

Parsley Purifier

Serves: 1 | Prep: 10–15 mins | Cook: none

Per serving : 152 CAL | 2.5G FAT | 0.2G SAT FAT | 22.1G CARBS | 9.7G SUGAR | 1.9G FIBER | 7G PROTEIN | 120MG SODIUM

As a diuretic, this drink really helps to cleanse your body. The strong flavors of the herbs and garlic are balanced by the natural sweetness of the sugar snap peas and the delicate flavor of the cucumber.

Ingredients

2 cups sugar snap peas

small handful of fresh
flat-leaf parsley

2 fresh rosemary sprigs

1 garlic clove

2 cups young spinach

½ cucumber

2 celery stalks, halved

1 teaspoon hempseed oil

chilled water, to taste

ice cubes, to serve (optional)

1. Feed the peas, parsley (reserving 1 sprig to garnish), rosemary, and garlic through a juicer, followed by the spinach, cucumber, and celery.

2. Pour into a glass and stir in the oil with water to taste.

3. Garnish with the reserved parsley sprig and serve with ice, if using.

Take a Fresh Look at Parsley

Parsley is rich in calcium and potassium, and it has loads of iron and phosphorus. Just 2 tablespoons of parsley contains 153 percent of the recommended daily allowance of vitamin K (which works with protein to strengthen bones).

Big Apple Detox

Per serving : 302 CAL | 1G FAT | 0.2G SAT FAT | 77.5G CARBS | 45G SUGAR | 4G FIBER | 2.7G PROTEIN | TRACE SODIUM

With its creamy, delicate parsnip and apple flavor fortified with cleansing ginger, this juice is perfect after an indulgent Thanksgiving or other holiday meal.

Ingredients
1 parsnip, halved
¼-inch piece of fresh ginger, peeled
2 apples, halved
⅓ cup chilled water
small handful of crushed ice (optional)

1. Feed the parsnip and ginger, then the apples, through a juicer. Top up with the water.

2. Fill a glass halfway with crushed ice, if using, then pour in the juice and serve immediately.

Fresh is Best

Instead of buying commercially made detox compounds or potions, juice fresh fruit and vegetables at home. Look at what you eat and when; you might find that making small changes will have a big impact. Ditch that high-calorie, full-fat coffee latte or cola and have a low-calorie, high-vitamin, and high-mineral juice instead.

Broccoli & Parsley Revitalizer

Serves: 1 | Prep: 10–15 mins | Cook: none

Per serving : 119 CAL | 0.6G FAT | 0G SAT FAT | 27G CARBS | 15.1G SUGAR | 0.2G FIBER | 3.2G PROTEIN | 80MG SODIUM

Ingredients

1⅔ cups large broccoli florets

small handful of fresh flat-leaf parsley

½ fennel bulb

2 apples, halved

chilled water, to taste

handful of crushed ice (optional)

1. Feed the broccoli and parsley, then the fennel and apples, through a juicer. Add water to taste.

2. Fill a glass halfway with crushed ice, if using, pour in the juice, and serve immediately.

Papaya & Apricot Soother

Serves: 1 | Prep: 15–20 mins | Cook: none

Per serving : 220 CAL | 1.3G FAT | 0.1G SAT FAT | 53.3G CARBS | 39.7G SUGAR | 6G FIBER | 4.1G PROTEIN | TRACE SODIUM

Ingredients

½ papaya, peeled, seeded, and coarsely chopped

4 apricots, halved and pitted

juice of 2 oranges

juice of 1 lime

small handful of crushed ice (optional)

¼ cup chilled water

1. Put the papaya, apricots, orange juice, and lime juice into a blender and blend until smooth.

2. Add the crushed ice, if using, and water and blend again until smooth.

3. Pour into a glass and serve immediately.

Why Not Try?

Celery is a good substitute
for fennel, but you will lose
the delicate anise flavor.

Fennel Flush

Serves: 1 | Prep: 10–15 mins | Cook: none

Per serving: 225 CAL | 1.5G FAT | 0.3G SAT FAT | 55.9G CARBS | 29.6G SUGAR | 4.3G FIBER | 7.4G PROTEIN | 200MG SODIUM

Fennel is a great source of fiber and contains potent antioxidants, which have been shown to reduce inflammation. Taking care of your insides will soon have you glowing on the outside.

Ingredients

3½ cups spinach

⅓ cup fresh mint

1 large fennel bulb, coarsely chopped

1 green apple, halved

1 lime, rind and pith removed, seeded, and coarsely chopped

crushed ice, to serve (optional)

1. Feed the spinach, mint, fennel, apple, and lime through a juicer.

2. Stir well and pour over the crushed ice, if using. Serve immediately.

Nettles

Nettles can sting (blanching in boiling water for a minute is one way to remove the sting), but including them in your diet will add valuable nutritional benefits. They are naturally high in iron, aiding red blood cell production for fending off diseases and infections and benefiting hair, skin, and nail health. Nettles are also incredibly high in calcium, promoting strong teeth and bones.

Green Tea

Green tea is known for containing a higher
concentration of vitamins than other foods
and beverages, making it incredibly valuable
for the body. It contains more than five
times the amount of folic acid found in
spinach, which is proven to decrease the
risks of colon cancer and dementia.
It also contains elements of GABA, an
acid that contributes to the lowering
of blood pressure.

Green Jump-Start

Serves: 1 | Prep: 10 mins | Cook: none

Per serving : 223 CAL | 1.3G FAT | TRACE SAT FAT | 51.4G CARBS | 35.6G SUGAR | 1G FIBER | 6.4G PROTEIN | 40MG SODIUM

You don't get a huge amount of juice from these green leaves, but what you do get is concentrated with antioxidants, minerals, and vitamins. Mix them with zucchini and apples for a health boost that will jump-start your detox.

Ingredients

2 cups young spinach

1 cup watercress or arugula

1 zucchini, halved

2 apples, halved

1 teaspoon wheatgrass powder (optional)

small handful of crushed ice (optional)

1. Feed the spinach and watercress, then the zucchini and apples, through a juicer.

2. Stir in the wheatgrass powder, if using.

3. Fill a glass halfway with crushed ice, if using, then pour in the juice and serve immediately.

Get into good habits

A detox can help you review your eating habits. Most of us don't eat enough green veg, and this tasty juice is a way to increase your consumption easily.

Bright Eyes

Serves: 1 | Prep: 15 mins, plus cooling | Cook: none

Per serving : 124 CAL | 0.5G FAT | TRACE SAT FAT | 31.4G CARBS | 21.9G SUGAR | 6.5G FIBER | 1.5G PROTEIN | 40MG SODIUM

Put a sparkle in your eyes with this delicious juice, which contains cleansing and antioxidant-rich green tea, carrot, apple, and parsley. Green tea and parsley are also thought to help improve aging eyesight.

Ingredients

⅓ cup boiling water

1 green tea bag, or 1 teaspoon green tea

1 carrot, coarsely chopped

1 apple, halved

small handful of fresh flat-leaf parsley

1–2 fresh flat-leaf parsley sprigs, to garnish

1. Pour the boiling water onto the green tea and let stand for 4 minutes. Strain and let cool slightly.

2. Put the carrot, apple, and parsley into a food processor or blender and process until smooth. Stir the juice into the tea.

3. Pour into a glass and serve warm or cold, garnished with parsley.

Green Tea Punch

Serves: 1 | Prep: 10–15 mins | Cook: none

Per serving: 62 CAL | 0.6G FAT | TRACE SAT FAT | 7.6G CARBS | 0.7G SUGAR | 2.6G FIBER | 6.8G PROTEIN | TRACE SODIUM

Green tea is packed with antioxidants. Combined with ginseng and wheatgrass, this is a great detoxifying juice that will cleanse you from the inside out.

Ingredients

1¼ cups green tea

juice of ⅓ lemon

¼ teaspoon liquid ginseng

1 teaspoon pea protein

1 teaspoon wheatgrass powder

1 teaspoon maca powder

ice cubes, to serve

1. Whisk the green tea with the lemon juice, ginseng, pea protein, wheatgrass powder, and maca powder. Alternatively, you could combine the ingredients in a blender.

2. Serve immediately over ice.

Beet Aid Detox

Serves: 1 | Prep: 10 mins | Cook: none

Per serving : 216 CAL | 1.1G FAT | 0.1G SAT FAT | 53.1G CARBS | 40.2G SUGAR | 5.9G FIBER | 5.9G PROTEIN | 200MG SODIUM

This ruby red juice looks more like a summer cocktail than an aid to detox. The inclusion of red chard boosts the antioxidant properties of its near relative, luscious beets, and the lime juice adds a zesty touch.

Ingredients

1 beet, halved

½ lime, rind and pith removed, seeded, and coarsely chopped

1 cup red Swiss chard

⅛ watermelon, thickly sliced and peeled

small handful of crushed ice (optional)

1. Feed the beet and lime, then the red Swiss chard and watermelon, through a juicer.

2. Fill a glass halfway with crushed ice, if using, then pour in the juice and serve immediately.

Health Notes

Beets contain almost all the
vitamins and minerals needed
to give your whole body a boost.
Watermelon's high water content
helps to rehydrate and plump
up your skin.

Why Not Try?

If you don't like celery, or just want to try something different, replace it with cucumber.

Rapid Recharge

Serves: 1 | Prep: 15 mins | Cook: none

Per serving : 200 CAL | 1.3G FAT | 0.2G SAT FAT | 48.3G CARBS | 36.4G SUGAR | 7.7G FIBER | 5.3G PROTEIN | 80MG SODIUM

Alfalfa sprouts contain high concentrations of calcium, vitamin K, and vitamin C, and give a great nutritional boost to this fresh-looking, cleansing green juice.

Ingredients

1 small zucchini, halved
1 celery stalk, coarsely chopped
1½ cups baby spinach
1¼ cups alfalfa sprouts
2 apples, peeled and cored
1 teaspoon alfalfa sprouts, to garnish

1. Put the zucchini into a blender with the celery. Add the spinach and alfalfa sprouts, then the apples.

2. Blend all the ingredients together, then pour into a glass.

3. Garnish with a few alfalfa sprouts and serve.

Fabulous Fennel

Fennel acts as a diuretic and has a
calming effect on the stomach while
providing useful amounts of
beta-carotene and folate.

Red Cabbage Digestive Aid

Serves: 1 | Prep: 15 mins | Cook: none

Per serving : 211 CAL | 0.8G FAT | 0.2G SAT FAT | 52.5G CARBS | 35.8G SUGAR | 2.9G FIBER | 5.7G PROTEIN | 120MG SODIUM

You will be amazed at the vibrant purple juice that comes from a red cabbage. This drink is light and aromatic, with a hint of cardamom (said to calm digestion) and the delicate sweetness of red grapes.

Ingredients

1 cup red grapes
½ fennel bulb
¼ head of red cabbage, coarsely chopped
3 cardamom pods
chilled water, to taste
small handful of crushed ice (optional)

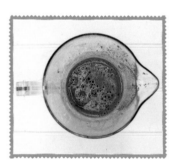

1. Feed the grapes, then the fennel, followed by the cabbage, through a juicer.

2. Coarsely crush the cardamom in a mortar with a pestle, discard the pods, and finely crush the black seeds, then stir them into the juice. Top up with water to taste.

3. Fill a glass halfway with crushed ice, if using, then pour in the juice and serve immediately.

Mother Earth

Coconut Restorer

Mother Earth

Serves: 1 | Prep: 10–15 mins | Cook: none

Per serving : 248 CAL | 15.7G FAT | 2.3G SAT FAT | 24.9G CARBS | 11G SUGAR | 10.6G FIBER | 5.5G PROTEIN | 80MG SODIUM

Ingredients

½ cup shredded curly green kale

1¼ cups chilled water

2 celery stalks, coarsely chopped

½ avocado, halved, pitted, flesh scooped from skin

1 small piece of turmeric root, peeled

1 tablespoon yuzu juice

1-inch piece fresh ginger, peeled

1 teaspoon bee pollen

1 tablespoon goji berries

1. Put the kale into a blender with the water and blend until smooth.

2. Chop the celery and avocado and add to the blender with the turmeric, yuzu juice, ginger, bee pollen, and goji berries.

3. Blend until smooth and serve immediately.

Coconut Restorer

Serves: 1 | Prep: 10–15 mins | Cook: none

Per serving : 162 CAL | 11.7G FAT | 4.4G SAT FAT | 11.4G CARBS | 4.5G SUGAR | 4.8G FIBER | 5.1G PROTEIN | 120MG SODIUM

Ingredients

½ cup shredded Tuscan or black-leaf kale

½ cup beet greens

1 teaspoon chia seeds

2 teaspoons almond butter

1 cup coconut milk

½ cup chilled water

pinch of chia seeds, to garnish

1. Put the shredded kale into a blender with the beets greens, chia seeds, and almond butter.

2. Pour in the coconut milk and water, then blend until smooth and creamy.

3. Serve immediately, sprinkled with chia seeds.

Healing Turmeric

Turmeric, a relation of ginger, has long been used in Chinese medicine to help treat depression. It is a natural antiseptic and antibacterial agent. However, it's the anti-inflammatory properties that may be of the most interest—they may help people with arthritis, soothe inflammatory skin infections, such as psoriasis, and—according to one study—help reduce the incidence of Alzheimer's disease.

Nature's Remedy

Serves: 1 | Prep: 10–15 mins | Cook: none

Per serving : 252 CAL | 0.8G FAT | 0.1G SAT FAT | 60.4G CARBS | 27.3G SUGAR | 3.8G FIBER | 4.9G PROTEIN | 80MG SODIUM

This drink tastes surprisingly mild, with a natural sweetness from the parsnip and carrots, and boy-oh-boy does it do you good.

Ingredients

2 carrots, halved

⅓ small onion, halved

1 garlic clove

1 parsnip, halved

1 orange, rind and a little pith removed, halved

¼ cup chilled water

pinch of ground turmeric

pinch of pepper

small handful of crushed ice (optional)

1. Cut a thin slice from a carrot and reserve.

2. Feed the remaining carrots and the onion, garlic, and parsnip, then the orange, through a juicer. Stir in the water, turmeric, and pepper.

3. Fill a glass halfway with crushed ice, if using, pour in the juice, garnish with the carrot slice, and serve.

Stress Buster

Serves: 1 | Prep: 15 mins | Cook: none

Per serving : 48 CAL | 0.3G FAT | 0G SAT FAT | 10.4G CARBS | 7.6G SUGAR | 0.1G FIBER | 1.1G PROTEIN | TRACE SODIUM

Ginseng is a natural stimulant that helps to combat stress and lifts the mood. This juice also aids liver and kidney function and prevents fluid retention.

Ingredients

1 ginseng tea bag or 1 teaspoon
ginseng tea

⅔ cup boiling water

1 apple, halved

2 cups arugula leaves

1. Put the tea into a cup, pour over the boiling water, and let stand for 4 minutes. Strain the water into a glass.

2. Feed the apple, then the arugula, through a juicer.

3. Stir the juice into the tea and serve warm or cold.

Dandelion Sunrise

Serves: 1 | Prep: 10–15 mins | Cook: none

Per serving : 287 CAL | 23G FAT | 7.9G SAT FAT | 16G CARBS | 3G SUGAR | 4.3G FIBER | 9.3G PROTEIN | TRACE SODIUM

Coconut butter is a spread made from the flesh of the coconut in the same way that peanuts are used to make peanut butter. It's packed with healthy fats and helps to keep you fuller for longer when added to smoothies.

Ingredients

½ cup dandelion greens

1 cup shredded curly green kale

1 cup chilled water

¼ cup cashew nuts

1½ teaspoons coconut butter

1 tablespoon sunflower seeds

1. Put the dandelion greens into a blender with the kale and water and blend until smooth.

2. Add the cashew nuts, coconut butter, and sunflower seeds and blend until smooth and creamy. Serve immediately.

Why Not Try?

Add 1 teaspoon of barley grass to help rid the body of toxins. Almonds or macadamia nuts would also work well in this recipe.

Green Goddess

Serves: 1 | Prep: 15 mins | Cook: none

Per serving : 71 CAL | 0.5G FAT | 0G SAT FAT | 14.3G CARBS | 11.5G SUGAR | 0.6G FIBER | 2.2G PROTEIN | 80MG SODIUM

This cooling, cleansing drink is good for liver and kidney function, helps lower cholesterol, and relieves tension and insomnia. It's high in iron and chlorophyll, which benefits your eyes and helps maintain healthy blood vessels.

Ingredients

½ Galia or honeydew melon,
thickly sliced and peeled

3 cups young spinach

2 large fresh
flat-leaf parsley sprigs

3 large fresh mint sprigs

small handful of crushed ice (optional)

1. Feed the melon, then the spinach, followed by the parsley and 2 mint sprigs, through a juicer.

2. Fill a glass halfway with crushed ice, if using, then pour in the juice.

3. Garnish with the remaining mint sprig and serve immediately.

Spinach Aid

Serves: 1 | Prep: 10–15 mins | Cook: none

Per serving: 23 CAL | 0.2G FAT | TRACE SAT FAT | 5.2G CARBS | 0.4G SUGAR | 0.5G FIBER | 1.3G PROTEIN | TRACE SODIUM

Dark and dreamy, this vibrant green shot packs a supercharge of goodness—for maximum benefit, don't leave a single drop in the glass.

Ingredients

¾ cup spinach
1 tablespoon aloe vera gel
juice of ½ lime
½ teaspoon spirulina powder
3½ tablespoons chilled water

1. Put the spinach, aloe vera, lime juice, and spirulina powder into a blender.

2. Pour in the water and blend until smooth. Serve immediately.

Index